JAN   2022

HE SAW THAT IT WAS GOOD

Praise for
He Saw That It Was Good

"Amisho has the courage to say what many are thinking and the candor to say what many are not. His words have positively influenced me for years—now this book gives the world that influence."

—LECRAE, artist

"I love my grandson so much. He is wise, sharp, and charming. I know his book will change many lives."
—LILLIE PRUITT, Sho's ninety-five-year-old grandmother, who has lived through the Jim Crow era, the Great Depression, the civil rights movement, and the Kobe and Shaq breakup

"This book is about the centrality of story for our identity and its power to transform vocation, art, and the church's witness. Sho does not shy away from the failures of White evangelicalism to affirm the fullness of the gospel story. But rather than 'canceling,' he shows how to tell a better story—embracing Black identity and Christian faithfulness. This book is a deep well of resources, inspired reflections on vocation and art making, and wisdom for cultural engagement. It is a gift to the church."
—TISH HARRISON WARREN, Anglican priest and author of
Liturgy of the Ordinary and *Prayer in the Night*

"Sho is one of the most strikingly original Christian thinkers of his generation. This book could not come at a better time. Ours is a time for courageous Christ-centered creativity. Sho rarely tells us what we want or expect to hear but speaks with artful poetry, fierce insight, and gracious justice about the issues of our era. I hang on his every word."

—TIMOTHY DALRYMPLE, PhD, president and CEO of *Christianity Today*

"Sho Baraka is the kind of cultural leader W. E. B. Du Bois and Frederick Douglass wanted for future generations: talented, thoughtful, critical, passionate, and gifted with a scholarly mind. That he is penning his thoughts to paper is a reverb of grace that should resound far and wide."

—DR. CHARLIE DATES, senior pastor of Progressive Baptist Church, Chicago

"Some voices are loud and others are widespread, but the voice of Sho Baraka is *solid*—and well worth listening to."

—DR. CARL ELLIS JR., author, theological anthropologist, and provost's professor at Reformed Theology Seminary

"Sho has not written a book for only creatives. He has written a book that will help all of us think intentionally about how the work we do (whatever it is) can be leveraged to fulfill God's purposes. It made me think about my own vocation with fresh eyes and how I can use my gifts to bring healing to our broken society. *He Saw That It Was Good* is the wonderful mix of history, theology, art, and cultural analysis that we need in this moment. I highly recommend it."

—ESAU McCAULLEY, PhD, assistant professor of New Testament at Wheaton College

"Amisho 'Sho' Baraka is one of the clearest voices of truth in this age of 'truth decay.' His insights, artistry, and intellect require that we embrace his truth, apply it, and follow as he leads us through this important work to a better future."

—C. JEFFREY WRIGHT, CEO and president of
UMI (Urban Ministries, Inc.)

"Throughout my ministry, I have leaned on many people. But when it comes to being both culturally relevant and doctrinally sound, I know no better man than my brother Sho. He has a prophetic edge and a pastoral tone. I am encouraged that he has finally decided to allow the world to get the knowledge I've been gleaning from him for the last forty years of my life."

—DHATI LEWIS, lead pastor of Blueprint Church
and vice president of Send Network

"I have been a fan of Sho Baraka's since first listening to his *Talented 10th* album. As a Du Bois scholar, I was intrigued by an artist with the breadth and depth to wrestle with race, politics, religion, and faith in a musical and deeply meaningful way. This book captures the unique tapestry of his richly textured life."

—BRIAN L. JOHNSON, PhD, president of Warner Pacific
University (former president of Tuskegee University)

"Sho has given us an apologetic for creative engagement in a culture that is losing its moral imagination. This book is both practical and artistic. I would highly recommend it."

—LISA FIELDS, president and founder of Jude 3 Project

"Sho Baraka is one of the most forward-thinking individuals I know, with the unique leadership quality to bring others up to his level. Engaging with his dynamic perspective in this book, we all get to level up, realizing something we never could on our own: that he saw it was good!"

—Tedashii, artist, author, actor, activist, and more

HE SAW THAT IT WAS GOOD

REIMAGINING YOUR CREATIVE LIFE
TO REPAIR A BROKEN WORLD

SHO BARAKA

Foreword by Chris Broussard

WATERBROOK

Library of Congress Cataloging-in-Publication Data
Names: Baraka, Sho, author.
Title: He saw that it was good: reimagining your creative life to repair a broken world / Sho Baraka.
Description: First edition. | [Colorado Springs, Colorado] : WaterBrook, an imprint of Random House, a division of Penguin Random House LLC, [2021]
Includes bibliographical references.
Identifiers: LCCN 2020054693 | ISBN 9780593193044 (hardcover) | ISBN 9780593193051 (ebook)
Subjects: LCSH: Creative ability—Religious aspects—Christianity. | Creation (Literary, artistic, etc.)—Religious aspects—Christianity. | Christianity and the arts.
Classification: LCC BT709.5 B36 2021 | DDC 261.5/7—dc23
LC record available at https://lccn.loc.gov/2020054693

Printed in Canada on acid-free paper

waterbrookmultnomah.com

2 4 6 8 9 7 5 3 1

First Edition

Interior book design by Susan Turner

SPECIAL SALES Most WaterBrook books are available at special quantity discounts when purchased in bulk by corporations, organizations, and special-interest groups. Custom imprinting or excerpting can also be done to fit special needs. For information, please email specialmarketscms@penguinrandomhouse.com.

For my Queen Patreece and the Royal Court:
Zoe, Zaccai, and Zimri. May we leave a legacy that is
easily reproduced but not easily forgotten.

BY CHRIS BROUSSARD

I first encountered Sho Baraka in 2004 while listening to Lecrae's debut album, *Real Talk*. Nestled in between the hard-hitting wordplay and "dirty South" bangers that lifted Lecrae to stardom was a melodic gem called "Tha Church" in which Sho introduced himself to hip-hop heads across the world. Though unknown, Sho shone like a quasar, rapping that he takes good news to "the streets, even in the alley schooling cats, quoting many facts."

Like any healthy organism, Sho has grown greatly since writing those rhymes. But anyone who has followed his journey over the past decade and a half knows that the last five words of that hip-hop quotable have come to define his career. Whether he's dropping a one-of-a-kind album that manages to simultaneously glorify God, celebrate African American heroes and heroines, and address America's vexing racial problem—all while making your head nod, of course—or he's dressed dapperly on the lecture circuit, Sho Baraka *schools*. And he schools with *facts*.

As I'm writing this, Sho's latest lesson over beats is *Their Eyes Were Watching*, an ode to the enslaved ancestors of African Americans and the liberating power of Jesus, who enabled many of them to sing spiritual masterpieces with hope and verve. In this album, Sho sounds like a hip-hop version of Richard Allen or George Washington Carver, vowing that White supremacy can neither cripple his soul nor hamper his creativity. In many ways, *He Saw That It Was Good* is *Their Eyes Were Watching* in book form.

In this canvas of a book, Sho takes you into his world—a place of honesty, transparency, grace, mercy, spirituality, victory, history, and humility. Oh, and, of course, as much as anything, *creativity*. At his core, Sho is an artist, and *He Saw That It Was Good* is both essay and poetry, literally and figuratively. While there are poetic stories that serve as interludes, the rhythm doesn't start or cease with them. Sho's writing style is musical. Better yet, it's jazz: unencumbered, sophisticated, forceful.

You will learn from this book. You will learn the power of stories—positive stories, negative stories, true stories, false stories, unspoken stories—and how they influence you and society. You will learn the power of identity—how it can cripple you when rooted in the wrong thing and bathe you in peace, love, and security when rooted in your Creator. You will learn the power of humility—how considering and understanding the viewpoints and circumstances of others can help you forgive, grow, and move on. You will learn the power of Black history when told from the perspective of equality and normalcy; for in this writing Sho doesn't shout from the rooftops and "announce with trumpets" that he's going to use Black stories, Black legends, and Black culture to bolster and illuminate truth to all people. He simply *does* it, like a White American might use Abraham Lincoln or the Revolutionary War when illustrating a point. It's the difference between teaching African American history during Black History Month and teaching it year-round alongside the record of other races and ethnicities, as if it's equal and supposed to be there. Trust me, it'll strike you.

And along the way, you will learn the power of creativity. You'll see how we rob ourselves and the world of beauty, joy, and wisdom when we shackle ourselves and others to cultural conformity. Sho teaches this from experience. I'm a witness that we are all better off to hear Sho's full and honest voice. Now in his rhymes, and in this book, Sho shares the good news in all its power and glory, testifying of the personal liberation that comes from the King, as well as the social implications that said freedom is intended to have on our world; you know, justice, freedom, equality, compassion . . .

Ever since Sho released his groundbreaking third studio album, *Talented 10th,* in 2013, I've been saying he should be as common and as recognized in traditional Black churches as Martin Luther King Jr. hand fans. Black preachers should use his music to teach congregants— particularly those who were raised on a diet heavy in hip- hop—the splendor of God's love and that the sky's the limit regardless of racism. Black professors in universities should use his work as a teaching tool when discussing the potency of art to celebrate and critique the Black condition, challenge the status quo, and speak truth to power.

And Black theologians should highlight his tracks as the hip-hop epitome of true Black liberation theology. No, he doesn't mimic James H. Cone but rather Absalom Jones, Sojourner Truth, and Henry Highland Garnet. As he once rapped, he is indeed "Frederick Douglass with a fade."

Sho's words, whether rapped or written, are the literary embodiment of the Black church. Combining the unswerving faith and evangelical fervor of the Church of God in Christ and scores of independent Black churches with the cries for biblical justice common to many well-heeled African Methodist Episcopal and Baptist churches, Sho brings the good news in all its fullness, application, and creativity. Regardless of your race, tradition, or background, when you're done reading this book (and perhaps rereading it), you and your soul will no doubt proclaim, "It was good."

CONTENTS

THE HIGHEST DIVINE

In a time now long forgotten, in a territory uncharted on our maps, lived a tribe of artisans. The people of the tribe trusted their eyes above all. Beauty and aesthetic were the currency of the land. Presentation was their beginning, and polish was their end.

The people of the tribe made it their tradition to sit in the grand company of the griots and poets. The raconteurs would tell many compelling tales. One that provoked much debate was a mysterious tale of the Highest Divine.

Not until the bronze bards could touch the still evening air did the people turn their ears to listen. The anticipation was long, like the sun climbing down into the desert's dusk. When the light and dark met perfectly in balance, the song began:

> *Of allure, of reverence, also in pride sat the chief,*
> *   as bearable as one wearing a crown could be.*
> *Prioritizing memories, not the present, his aim*
> *   gentle, not for charity's sake but for his own name.*
> *His imagination soared. His veneer blocked the skies*
> *   in plumage beautifully arranged; he lusted for eyes.*
> *Many honors he held, yet one he could not own:*
> *   to make his name eternal and outlive his throne.*
>
> *A decree caressed the mountains and kissed the*
> *   barren flats,*
> *   tempting the skilled to a spurious act.*

The chief knew his tribe loved the gods above all,
  and to build idols of gods was the highest call.
He sought to find favor with such a request
  that though he may die, in memories he would rest.
"Paint the image of the Highest Divine.
And ere'where thy kingdom stands, thy face shall fly."

His seat was swarmed. Works, both fair and foul—
  none were shy, neither adult nor child.
Behold a brave soul kneeling before the royal line,
  hoped to bring rapture in painting the Highest
    Divine.
The painting evoked the mystery of the Divine's nature
  of fire, of spirit, of water, of vapors.
The face was absent, but the presence bold—
  the proudest cloud would envy the complex mold.
Though it had courage and precision in craft,
  the chief found it a puzzle, familiar to daft.
It took no form like kings and queens,
  lacking splendor. The chief was not pleased.

Then approached another with craft on trial,
  aiming to raise the sun to a smile.
The Highest Divine was peaceful and still,
  a giver of life and a healer of ills.
The painting was spangled with love and fertility.
Surely the Highest Divine knows civility.
The chief loved her meekness; her face was quite kind
  but much too soft to be Lord in his time.
Though her welcome was warm and her invite was
    wide,
  he could not see this work as the Highest Divine.

While defeat escorted many, at the throne waited chance
    to acknowledge the work of an artisan's hands.
A portrait presented a soul lacking fear,
    wearing conquest like braids, tossing flames like spears.
Aggression in grin, dominion in laughter,
    requiring praise from palace to pasture.
The chief had no quarrel with his enemies' fate,
    but that alone does not a Highest Divine make.

Just before the sun set on the ambitious decree
    came one last portrait for the chief to see.
The craftsman presented it with elated belief,
    for he knew his work would please the chief.
He removed the veil for the spectators' eyes,
    endorsing vanity with fawning surprise.
"Mansa, if you seek imagery of the Highest above,
    why turn our gaze from the chief whom we love?
    Thy rule is a lion; thy face is a lily.
    Thy name will be praised from city to city."

His smile mimicked the sun; his eyes were ivory tusk—
    he as the Highest Divine, his solitary lust.
Forever immortal, his image in the heavens.
Nor death, nor successor will erase his reverence.

The chief now is in the company of gods.
Few in the tribe found his praise to be odd.
Lo, all did not swoon before the portrait and lie;
    the wife of the artist had just and true eyes.

She honored the chief and knew the work of his
*   hands,*
*   but why make him a deity? She did not understand.*
She knew purity and piety, and this she did not laud.
"Though your soul is beautiful, love, you paint an
*   insufferable God."*

THE GOOD LIFE

I'ma test this out right quick on y'all
Now keep in mind that I'm an artist and I'm
sensitive . . .

—ERYKAH BADU

By the grace given to me I say to everyone
among you not to think of himself more highly
than he ought to think, but to think with sober
judgment, each according to the measure of faith
that God has assigned.

—ROMANS 12:3

We discover an immeasurable amount of good in our
lives when we truly realize the depths of our depravity and indifference. We would each like to think we are
part of the solution rather than the problem. However, our
story is, of course, more complicated.

There are degrees to how we contribute to the decay of
society. Passivity and avarice are dangerous contagions.

We fall prey to them when we assume that our lives and work have no adverse impact on the people around us. Add to that assumption our arrogance in thinking our ideology is inevitably right, and we have . . .

. . . A *problem*. So before I begin to talk about how we can each richly contribute to the flourishing of a blessed society, let's get centered. Let's see ourselves rightly, not thinking of ourselves more highly than we ought. Only then will we know our real ability to give *good* to those around us.

What is good? How do we center our creative contributions? God has told us what is good. Those good instructions are "to do justice, and to love kindness, and to walk humbly with your God."[1] He gave more instructions too—"love the Lord your God with all your heart and with all your soul and with all your strength and with all your mind, and your neighbor as yourself."[2]

These instructions have two facets: inward devotion and outward duty. The Christian faith is one both of mind and of body. It is cognitive and corporeal. No one is excused from these commands.

The command to love—in all the fullness and justice of that word—is laid on all, from politician to painter. With every policy pushed, every stroke of the brush, we put forth what we believe about God and about good. With what we make, we affect the world. For better or for worse.

To build a good culture, you need a good memory. To be a good artist, you honor the past and learn from those before you. Strangely, this sense of where our culture has been sets us free to chart our course into the future. *There is nothing new under the sun* . . . , except those who are renewing their minds under the Son. When "progress" rejects the past, we all lose.

In this book, I am sharing from my journey of integrating past, present, and progress. We all want our work to matter. We all want to create from a deep place, a *good* place. And this is how we start well: It should be a daily practice to look back with wisdom while looking forward with optimism. That perspective helps us ask the important questions: *How can knowing history help me make better contributions tomorrow? Do I use my work for good, or is the outcome avarice, shame, or demoralization?*

Each of us is creative. Each of our lives becomes a canvas displaying what our idea of good is. But without humility, we make terrible gods. The same talent that can help us shape the world for Christ can be used to carve dark idols. We all live with an image of the Chief of the tribe. Sometimes that image is just a slightly bigger effigy of ourselves. We all have gold and shadow—the light and the dark sides of our creativity. We are all like Miss Badu in that we carry a bit of sensitivity about our work, beliefs, and identity. We desire to create a world that would honor and protect those aspects of us. That desire is often admirable, but our methods can be dangerous.

The creative life seeks to produce or restore the blessings of a truth that benefits more than just ourselves. It seeks to reform our souls and society. It recognizes the evils around us while not allowing them to paralyze us. To do this work well, we must always be doing inventory on our hearts and hands. *Why* are we making, and *what* are we making? The creative life honors the Spirit that inspires us while fixing our eyes on a redemptive future in which God has invited us to participate.

Again—we *all* are creative in some way or another. No matter the work, it can contribute to the good of society. But we still need to ask how we can fully live into our creative calling, how we can find transcending principles that will help mature our creative life.

And that is what this book is all about. If I can make it plain, as my dad would say, "All money ain't good money." Dare I say it?

All work ain't good work.

I live in America—a beautiful and messy motley of tribes tossed into a melting pot. The minorities of this country have historically been the fuel used to heat the pot— burned up to keep the whole thing cooking. But in this cruel crucible, creativity and goodness have managed to take root. The image of the Creator has been glimpsed, often where those in power would never think to look.

The griots* and singers, preachers and prophets of these marginalized tribes have given us an imagination that could make this place better. We cannot ignore their work. We use our past and present to form our future. We hope to construct a new normal with truth and righteousness. We are new griots and prophets sent to speak new tongues, tell new stories, and present new ideas.

* A storyteller, bard, and poet in some West African traditions.

My social and spiritual liberation is accredited to the artists and movements that left a legacy before me. I learned old poems and turned them into raps. I heard Negro folklore and flipped them into new narratives. These individuals showed me how their faith and art could bring benefit and pleasure to the world in chaos. I praise God for his Spirit working through creation.

You do not have to be a scholar to contribute to the ongoing scrutiny of racism and other ills in American history. Most rational people will admit that it is filled with vileness and the abuse of power. However, a debate rages in society as to whether or not those historical ills have any real detrimental effects today. Should institutions or individuals in history be placed on a scale to see whether their good work outweighs their evil? How are we to judge and honor individuals in retrospect when values and virtues evolve?

I reminisce on the spring of 2017 when I was the lone westerner in a cypher of African minds brilliantly dialoguing about global issues. The rhythm of the conversation moved from African identity to Black American privilege to colonization. The rhythm would soon shake the foundation of a historical figure I hardly viewed as troublesome. That historical figure was Shaka kaSenzangakhona, better known in the West as Shaka Zulu. Shaka Zulu is mostly known to the West as an innovative war chief of the Zulu tribe who demanded the respect of colonizing Europeans.

However, one of the bright minds in the room began to critique Shaka as a colonizer himself. Many scholars and armchair critics charge him with enslavement, devastating the tribal population, and slaying pregnant women and their husbands in psychotic rage after the death of his mother.[3]

I'm sure Shaka believed his work was noble. Some people, in history and today, would agree. There is an airport in Durban named in his honor, as well as an amusement park. Scholars debate the details and legacy of his life. It's completely reasonable how the oppressed people in South Africa created a heroic narrative around a historical figure who would affirm their inherent dignity even if that individual moved with a looming shadow. We celebrate his gold in battle while ignoring the shadow of his tribalism. I experienced no emotional trauma when laying my eyes on the airport or amusement park bearing his name while I visited Durban. However, I imagine someone does. Everyone's hero has the potential to be a villain to others. Work that seems good to you may be a curse to others. We must understand the complex composition of our lives. We have the propensity to be both heroes and villains. It is very possible for you to be an oppressor and a liberator.

This forever shifted my idea of cancel culture. We sing the songs and praises of David. We read the gems of Paul. However, I'm sure Uriah's relatives felt anger at the very mention of the king. I'm sure the family members of those persecuted by Paul had some contempt for his letters.

Individuals are complex, and their legacies are complicated. How we tell their stories can have a bigger impact than the bloodshed itself. Those stories have a very real possibility of contributing to future bloodshed. In the wake of the emancipation, if the stories told by the South (with the aid of Northern political expediency) had been better, America would most likely have a better racial union. Legacies wouldn't have been embellished, and bigotry would not have found a home in public policies.

I dare not make any false equivalence, but I must also recognize that some of my favorite thinkers can be chided for their shadows. G. K. Chesterton was hesitant to support the suffrage movement.[4] Alexander Crummell held discriminatory views of Native Americans.[5] Martin Luther King Jr. was outed by the FBI as a womanizer.[6] W. E. B. Du Bois wrote a glowing eulogy for Joseph Stalin despite his atrocious war crimes.[7] We should not ignore the shadows of those we love. This is not an endorsement or a condemnation of iconoclasm, but I hope it's a sober reminder that we are messy people living in a messy society. When our humility is low, our anger is high and we are certain our ideology is right; we are capable of doing substantial damage.

As you actively engage the coming chapters, I hope you think critically about your own life. How do you define *good*? How does that definition compare with the Bible's grand narrative of creation, redemption, and justice? How have stories shaped your identity? Do you contribute to biblical liberation or cultural restriction? Do you live with fear and pessimism or with empowerment? Is your faith one that incorporates the mind and body, self and community? What does it mean to be centered in a culture that lives in the extremes?

As we acknowledge our propensity to vacillate between extremes, our earnest prayer is that the gospel of Jesus Christ will center us. There is a reason God gave us repentance. That repentance aims to repair the societal brokenness created by others and ourselves. We do not have a faith that is selfish.

This book wrestles with the complexity of humanity and finds redemption in the dysfunction. It is a book that wants to recalibrate us. All told, I think this is a book about honesty.

There is much to mourn in this world and in myself. But I have resolved that I will not live in despair. Nor will the deplorable acts of the past define me. My present is centered in a redemptive narrative. My future is full of hope. And I pray you have similar resolutions.

I stand here because of the resilience and hope of those heroes who've gone before me:

The organizational skills of Richard Allen.
The leadership of Harriet Tubman.
The passion of David Walker.
The intellect of Anna Julia Cooper.
The imagination of Phillis Wheatley.
The foresight of Alexander Crummell.
The wisdom of Frederick Douglass.
The creativity of George Washington Carver.

The courage of Fannie Lou Hamer.

The relevance of Tom Skinner.

Jesus walked with them. He walks with me.

He walks with you.

And I believe that, together, our creative life can repair this broken world.

Will you join me?

HE SAW THAT IT WAS GOOD

1

YOU LOOK GOOD IN RED

Tell your children of it,
and let your children tell their children,
and their children to another generation.

—Joel 1:3

*I*nheritance.

What my grandfather left, my father gave to me. What my father left, I have to bequeath to my children.

But what I pass on to my children is more than wealth (or debt) or these Adonis-like features. Inheritance is about more than those things. I pass on ideas. I pass on virtues. I pass on values that help form their concepts about the world.

What others pass to us shapes how we see the world. It shapes how we see *ourselves*. When I was an impressionable young boy, my mother once told me I looked good wearing the color red. At that point in my life, I didn't have much fashion sense. I didn't know which colors I hated or which I loved. But I cared about what my mother said. It carried weight. Suddenly *I looked good in red*. That was more than a compliment. It was a scientific truth.

But the story doesn't stop there. I grew up in Southern California, in a suburban community that was known as a Crip neighborhood. Wearing red was more than simply matching colors or exercising your freedom to explore the color wheel—to the wrong eyes, it meant an affiliation with the Crips' rival gang, the Bloods. In the wrong spot, red could get you in serious trouble.

Looking back, I wonder at the power of my attachment to the color red. I've had friends killed because of gang violence—many of them with no gang affiliation. Wrong place, wrong time. In hindsight, I could have died more than once for wearing the wrong color. But I was willing to be confronted, picked on, and insulted because of a simple affirmation that my mother spoke to my adolescent imagination. *I looked good in red.* To this day, if you ask my favorite color, I'll tell you "Red."

If our lives are music, stories are the instruments that arrange it. A simple compliment from my mother quietly became a *story* I heard about myself. A story that shaped how I lived, including the risks I took to believe that story, to act on it. It became an image for how a simple word can shape someone's world.

Today I am a storyteller. I am employed for my imagination. In my art and performance, I can construct worlds. I can rearrange reality. I can tell the truth. My vocation is a vessel, allowing me, in a way, to time travel. Part of this storytelling work is learning the stories that have already been told, both good and bad. Part of the work is trying to understand how our culture and faith and very lives have been shaped by the words of others. I dig for the gold of the past. I also try to trace its shadows. And in both the light and the dark, I am learning about myself, about *us* today.

To be a good storyteller, you must first be an honest observer. No matter what you're cooking, honesty is the best ingredient.

History is about telling narratives. And the honest communication of those narratives has the power to shape our future. But there's more than one way to get a story wrong. Popular historian Howard Zinn critiqued the way many historians mismanage the past: "One can lie outright about the past. Or one can omit facts which might lead to unacceptable conclusions."[1] Both can result in misshapen stories.

This book is about many things. But at the core it's about how the stories we live shape the world around us. How we can use our creativity to bring gold or shadow into reality. There is no word or story too small to matter. Not mine. Not yours. But like the power of my mother's compliment—*"You look good in red"*—we must consider the power of the narratives we live.

Stories have the ability to cultivate societies. Or to kill them. The ethnic lies accepted by the Hutu and Tutsi peoples in Rwanda (lies engineered by German colonizers generations before) were the roots that gave rise to the 1994 genocide that killed over eight hundred thousand human beings.

So, as we embark on this journey, let's start by considering our stories.

The story seed that rooted the Hebrew people was

planted in one of the first stories of the Bible—the Garden of Eden. After God made the cosmos, what he said about humanity is one of the most profound statements possible about our identity: *"Let us make humankind in our image."*[2] From the beginning, God saw us to be evidence of his existence. His *image*. Furthermore, God blessed that image by stating that we are "very good."[3]

He saw that it was good. In that simple statement, we can find our beginning and our purpose. And this purpose begins with us being like God. These are positive affirmations. His creation would start running the marathon of existence knowing they have dignity, purpose, and support. Our heads are up, our eyes are focused, and our hearts are filled with confidence. We have been given a gift that is priceless and a world in which to use it for God's glory for all eternity.

But if only it were that easy. Of course, it isn't. Because of sin, the creative impulse can be cloaked in shadow. A simple story can be a seed that grows and produces the manifestations of evil deeds.

We are shaped by our stories, and we are given our stories by our tribes. There are no blank slates. We get our gold and shadow, our centering, and our creative life from our tribes.

We each belong to a tribe in some capacity. Our tribal associations span the spectrum from nations to families. But no matter what tribe you come from, one thing is constant. *Every* group is fashioned by a story.

What is the story of your tribe? It's one of the most important questions to ask. The answer has likely defined you long before you were aware of it.

The stories we accept about our tribes have lasting impact on how we see ourselves. In my song "Kanye, 2009," I made an observation about the common mistake of tethering African American identity to slavery:

> *Why does Black history always start with slavery*
> *so even when I'm learning, they're still putting those*
> *chains on me?*[4]

Do you follow? To believe my identity as a Black man starts as a seed sprouted from the ground of slavery suffocates my dignity. It tells me something false about my purpose. Is oppression what defines my narrative? If oppression is at the center of my formation, then the implications of that oppression will inform what I love, who I love, and how I love. Until new stories are told, your whole identity is in bondage.

The deepest roots of my story matter. What if there is a deeper truth about me? Something that runs beyond generational pain into something richer and older and more beautiful?

Even the shadows of our stories are powerful. In our search for honesty, it's possible to cultivate pessimism or even self-contempt, *if* we don't go back to the true beginning of our narrative—made in the image of God. Made to help create the world. Able to tell a better tale to anyone who will listen. Able to be liberated and to help Jesus liberate others from the stories that confine and oppress. My identity is not chained to the oppressive actions of any nation or individual. Neither is yours. If we let that happen, we lose our rightful gold in the shadows of a small and dangerous story.

As we understand our creative potential as image bearers of God, *we need to understand our stories.* Especially the stories of our tribes. In *Outliers,* Malcolm Gladwell popped one stereotyped story by observing that people of Asian descent aren't good at math because of genetics. Rather, a common cultural or family disposition to work hard tends to create communities of students who value hard work and excel in the classroom.[5]

Frank Smith, an expert on language and formation, would call this learning process "the classic view of learning." It holds that "we learn from people around us with whom we identify."[6] This means we are learning even when we aren't aware of it.

Those "people around us" make up our tribes. The tribes we belong to teach us how to paint God. They shape our values and imagination. They give us the colors . . . the canvas . . . the backdrop . . . that we apply to our creativity, to our liberty, to our shaping of a good life. One tribe's God might look like a 1970s hippie. Another tribe's God may be fashioned like a Maasai warrior.

As part of our growth, we all have to begin questioning the stories we were given about ourselves, about the world, about God. We have to compare what we've inherited with the stories Jesus told about a humanity being redeemed. What does your tribe say about the poor? What does it say about sex and relationships? Whether you come from a conservative village or a progressive metropolis, odds are that you have assumptions about your narrative. How might those assumptions be shaping your creative life right now? How might they be imprisoning you? And most important—*how do they compare with God's image in you?*

Storytelling isn't always intentional. In fact, it's often most powerful when it's not—like my mother's simple comment that I look good in red.

Many of us are blind to the storytelling we do as we travel through our personal narrative arc. The decisions we make communicate our beliefs about the world. But do we see the story? Rarely. But we are still living out a story—a plot with setting, characters, conflict, and (maybe) resolution. We are participating in the creation of our narrative, either passively or actively.

The question we must ask ourselves is, *What is the story I'm telling with my life and work?* Or asked another way, *How do my life and work paint what I believe about God?* You see, we live the story we believe. If we passively float through life, reacting only to the actions of others, our story is likely to be far from its full potential. But if we believe what God said about us, how we were made in the image of the Creator himself—well, wouldn't that change everything? Wouldn't that set us free to live our true story, our true creative life?

Great stories have heroes and villains. In the myths and movies, it's usually easy to tell the difference. But the stories of human life are usually more complex. Here our character is not fixed, as in a comic book, but is shaped by the acts we do in our daily lives. Many of us are both part of the problem and part of the solution. Part of the broken world and part of the hope of new life that can help heal it.

The book of Romans states, "There is no one righteous, not even one."[7] This is the human condition. We all can become the very thing we fight against. The economist can advise a company toward great financial gains while ignoring the effect her work will have on the poor. The activist for justice can be so consumed with outrage that he slowly slips into a version of the moral despotism he opposes. The theologian can conveniently emphasize principles in her teachings that fit comfortable cultural norms while ignoring points that challenge them.

Cartoons and comic books benefit from caricatures of heroes and villains. They are simple stories. Kids have limited capacity to interpret the abstract. We need to make it clear to them who the bad guy is, so we drape him in dark colors, make him unpleasant to the eye, and give him a sinister lair and few redeeming qualities.

But in real life, if evil were so easily discernable, no one would fall for it. In the real world, heroes cast shadows. Villains can have admirable qualities. (Just read the stories of Moses, David, or Solomon in the Bible.) We ourselves can blur the line between the two with how we think, act, worship, and create. We swing constantly between the reverent and the repentant, between living in the big story of God's good image and in the many smaller, twisted stories that we've been told since Eden.

If an honest story is the foundation of how we understand ourselves, then it's also the starting point for living and creating as people made in the image of God. But keeping our stories honest is almost as tough as finding the true story in the first place.

One of the great obstacles to telling an honest story is *manipulation*. As a child, I would sometimes manipulate stories because of my deep desire to be in the middle of the action. It's embarrassing now, but I would sometimes lie about being present at events I was nowhere near. Someone would ask, "Did you hear about so-and-so?" and I'd respond with details I either heard or invented, believing they would add to my overall plot. It was not that I enjoyed lying in the least. I enjoyed being involved. I wanted to feel important. My manipulated scripting helped satisfy my social yearnings. (I outgrew the bad habit!) In those early, awkward retellings, I was experimenting with how it felt to shape a story.

Of course, the stakes in such manipulation can be much higher. We see this in the words of a certain snake in the first chapters of Genesis. The serpent retold a very important story—*just* close enough to the original to be recognizable but with the key details all twisted. Satan told Adam and Eve a dishonest story about their self-importance in the ecosystem of Eden. Satan intoxicated them with ideas of their own supremacy—suddenly they were the central characters, and God was a withholding villain.

You will be like gods . . .

The irony is that Adam and Eve already had what the snake was lying about. They had intrinsic immortality that would soon be jeopardized because of their desire to stand equal with their Creator. Their identity was perfectly sufficient already. They had been made in God's own image. They had been invited to fill the world with him through their creativity and productivity. But after the serpent started talking, it wasn't enough.

And isn't that the core of our temptation? To put ourselves at the center of the story while pushing others to the margins. While we are hoarding spaces, we fail to recognize that there is enough affirmation for us all. Our disobedience is the product of impulses detached from God. Self-interest seeking satisfaction. This is precisely what happens when peripheral players attempt to replace the main character in the story—which always has been and always will be God.

When we lose the story, we lose ourselves.

In 2012, I found myself at a creative and spiritual crisis. At one point during that year, I was in New York City, attending an IAM (International Arts Movement) conference. I was searching for meaning in my creative calling.

During that time, I began to see that I'd been working

from an incomplete story. What I believed about theology was affecting how I created. I began to realize that my work held a theological pessimism, and it was beginning to ring hollow.

The Christian message that I was taught as a young man stressed sin and brokenness. The point was clear—humanity had sinned, and Jesus was acting to redeem. A true story! But not the *whole* story. I realized that a gospel story that begins in the New Testament makes our activity the primary problem. But when I went back to Genesis? It was our *identity* that was the primary problem. And our deepest identity?

He saw that it was good.

Now, sin's vital to talk about. We need to be (kindly) reprimanded for our failures. But is our failure the whole story? No. And if we believe it is, we are in danger of being manipulated. The recipients of our message can easily be misled—by their own misunderstanding—to believe that the message of redemption is about performance. About doing. The story has gone wrong!

The roots of our identity are so much deeper! We are made in the image of a righteous and creative God, and Jesus is restoring that fallen image through his redemption. But that restoration often means we have to examine the stories we've believed.

In Matthew 19, Jesus was approached by a rich young ruler who had a question about eternal life. After Jesus told him to keep the commandments, the young man let him know that he had. Yeah, he *had* kept the requirements of the law. The rich young ruler believed this pious faithfulness, this performance, should grant him entrance into the kingdom. From the outside, his story seemed to be right on track.

But Jesus saw through this man's righteous activity into his heart. And the narrative there was different. Jesus gave him a command that would challenge everything he identified with. Jesus told the rich young ruler, "If you want to be complete, go and sell your possessions and give to the poor, and you will have treasure in heaven; and come, follow Me."[8] The man left distraught. Why? His story had been shaken. He was unwilling to abandon whatever narrative he had constructed about himself to follow after Jesus. No matter how good-natured or wealthy he was, Jesus had implied that his *identity* was incomplete.

Our creative life isn't just about what we do. It's about who we are. I believe the gospel isn't just a redemption of our activity; it is ultimately a redemption of our *identity*. If we never tell our deepest story honestly, then we can never truly reform.

In the Georgia community where I live and work, I don't have to convince people that they are sinful or that the world is broken. We can see it around us. Humanity is fragile. Our inability to uphold a righteous moral code is obvious. Our shortcomings show themselves in crime, questionable government policies, malignant marketing, and fractured relationships. Look out the window. The story's all twisted.

Our challenge is to believe the other side of the equation. We need to accept that our humanity has intrinsic worth—a goodness far beyond the self-centered gratification we experience in everyday activity. Our deepest identity is *good*. I am committed to spreading this part of our deeper narrative because I know how powerful it is for our beliefs and our creativity.

This shift in worldview forever changed me. I no longer see the gospel as a weapon that forces people to confess their moral criminality. We've gotten it all backward. Sure, confession of sin is necessary. But I see the gospel as a portrait—a picture of God's own image that offers a return to our intended wholeness. Once we see a flawless portrait, we will see the deficiency in our own paintings. Then true confession will overflow because we see the deeper goodness that our sin holds us back from.

Art is not a tool for evangelistic chastisement. Too often Christians have used creativity as a tool for tearing down when it was always meant as a tool for construction. The question becomes, Will we be able to build with an honest vision of our deepest identity in God?

For our Creator *saw that it was good*.

Dishonest stories haphazardly paint bull's-eyes on the backs of others. The transmission of tropes and harmful ideologies can have a massive impact on how people view themselves and their world, especially when the targets don't have equal opportunity to form narratives. In *Toms, Coons, Mulattoes, Mammies, and Bucks*, Donald Bogle detailed how Hollywood has perpetuated negative racial tropes.[9] These caricatures have been a cultural pillar to help uphold racial injustice in America. Many people today would be shocked to discover how Negro dehumanization in the false narratives of vaudeville and Hollywood fueled and funded much of America's early entertainment.

In the early nineteenth century, minstrel shows were America's preeminent entertainment contribution to the world. It's significant that this country's entertainment was built on degradation and bigotry. Which makes me ask, How can we expect honest stories to come from a machine that was built on radical racial dishonesty? We are still feeling the effects of that dishonesty today.

Our world shapes the stories we tell. Then the stories we tell shape our world. Narratives that are successful entertainment are also beneficial for politicians. Why? *Because they shape how we see ourselves.* In the late nineteenth and early twentieth centuries, negative Black stereotypes leaped from the vaudeville stages onto the campaign trail, with responses changing from laughter to angry jeers. They depicted the newly freed Negro as lazy and ignorant. Negroes were not the only victims of cruel and cartoonish portrayals. Immigrants were harshly satirized to promote political agendas. Chinese workers were depicted as violent and filthy. The Irish were cast as primates and political radicals. Women who supported suffrage were consistently painted as unloved, manly, and unattractive.

Dishonest narratives are employed because when comfort or tradition is threatened, it is not enough to challenge a legitimate political or social stance. Rather, you must dehumanize your opposition. You can sway opinion by exaggerating differences. And you can do it not with civil debate or discussion but with *stories*.

Dangerous narratives come in many forms. But they all shape our identity. In American storytelling, you can learn a lot from what the story line neglects to mention. Our identity is not always formed by what is directly inserted into a narrative. We are also formed by what is omitted.

Black people, among other minorities, have often been shaped by these omissions. In his book *The Mis-Education of the Negro,* Carter G. Woodson quoted an abolitionist as saying, "The portrait of the Negro has seldom been drawn but by the pencil of his oppressor and the Negro has sat for it in the distorted attitude of slavery."[10] The point? That often the minority story is secondhand—and distorted.

Certainly, dysfunctional systems and racist ideologies are to blame for this. Yes, our world is broken. *But we must look inward and realize that no matter who we are, we have the ability to tell a better story.* We have been created to create. We have power—from the image of God—to challenge these omissions in the most beautiful ways.

I remember reading these liberating words from my favorite novelist, Toni Morrison:

> [The] function of racism . . . is distraction. It keeps you from doing your work. It keeps you explaining, over and over again, your reason for being. Somebody says you have no language, and so you spend twenty years proving that you do. Somebody says your head isn't shaped properly, so you have scientists working on the fact that it is. Somebody says that you have no art, so you dredge that up. . . .

None of that is necessary. There will always be one more thing.[11]

These distractions can create an identity of pessimism. We begin to turn the pen against ourselves. Our music becomes jaded, then misogynistic and unnecessarily violent. Colorism runs rampant in our films and social settings. Anti-intellectualism can be praised in lower-income communities. Furthermore, White supremacy becomes a troll of the mind, obstructing our bridge to every conceivable opportunity. No matter our background—but especially if we are from communities whose stories have been oppressed or omitted—we *must* believe in the power of our pens. In our ability to use our creativity to truly change things—even if the horizons are small.

I say let these false narratives drown with the ships that brought them across the Atlantic. There is a better way, and I mean to live it.

When my daughter was seven years old, she approached me and said that she did not like her hair or skin color. I was caught off guard. I'd hoped this was a scenario we would never have to experience. My wife and I *constantly* affirm our children's beauty and intelligence. My daughter sees affection and affirmation reciprocated in her parents' marriage. We've been told that our house is nothing short of an African American museum with a plethora of Black art and images displayed. We have done our best to tell a full story about that skin color, about the beauty and heritage of that hair. She had attended a school that was 99 percent African American. I knew we were raising a secure and confident girl. With our hard work to celebrate her unique beauty, I'd hoped we would avoid the messaging that could prompt disgust about it.

After making her watch seventy-two hours (I'm joking—it was eighty-two hours!) straight of *Eyes on the Prize, Roots,* and *Doc McStuffins* without sleep, food, or water, I began to investigate the cause of the dilemma. Do you know what I began to realize? That no matter how much affirmation my daughter received from her parents or school, we couldn't avoid the overwhelming and biased stories in popular culture.

My daughter was struggling to see beauty in something dismissed by or invisible to so much of the rest of the world. I learned that she is being formed and informed by voices all around, many of which are telling and selling incomplete narratives. From cartoons to merchandising, stories were being told—so constantly and urgently that even the environment of our home could not be a perfect shelter.

Identity formation is not a closed gate but a revolving door. Many times we are unaware of who enters the corridors to instruct us. But neither are we aware of the impact of *our* contributions. The power of our own creative impact on the world. We don't always see it—at least not immediately—but that doesn't mean it's not there.

In February 2018, the world was introduced to Marvel's film adaptation of the comic *Black Panther.* The film quickly became a cultural phenomenon. Critics and fans alike praised the movie—and it went on to become the third-highest-grossing film of all time in the United States. But it was more than just a film. Across the globe, the movie became a celebration of the Black diaspora. People caught a vision.

Not only did the opening week boast high attendance, but it also became an atmosphere for cosplay and Afrofuturism. It was the first time I had ever witnessed a mass movement of Black moviegoers participating in costume, *joining* the story they were there to see. A mythical country in Africa called Wakanda suddenly felt like a real place.

It was all the more astonishing when compared with films like *The Last of the Mohicans, The Last Samurai, The Great Wall,* and *Dances with Wolves.* Those past blockbusters had spotlighted an indigenous or "other" people group but centered a White male lead. The choice was naive—and it was harmful. While honoring another culture on the surface, Hollywood had embraced the belief that Whiteness must be centered (and heroic) in order for consumers to care.

Of course, *Black Panther* struck back hard at that assumption. But for me, what is most significant about this film is not the 2018 smash. It's what took place about fifty years before.

It was 1966. America was fresh off the heels of the Civil Rights Act and still consumed with the Vietnam War. One year after the death of el-Hajj Malik el-Shabazz (Malcolm X) and two years before the death of Martin Luther King Jr.

In the midst of political and racial turmoil, two brave gentlemen figured it might benefit the world (and their profits, I assume, as not all good work is charity) to create a comic book hero from an African nation. It was a creative risk. This Black protagonist would defend his country against supervillains and White supremacists. Stan Lee and Jack Kirby, two White men, had the courage to give the comic book world a hero like they had never seen. It would be fifty years before that choice had the impact we all felt, but they made it. They told a better story.

Telling honest stories takes courage. And we never know what the outcome of that creative bravery will be.

In January 2013, I released an album titled *Talented 10th*. This was my first solo project after my departure from Reach Records. My departure was already something of a stumbling block for those who couldn't comprehend why I would leave such a successful record label. (I will speak more about that departure in chapter 5.)

Talented 10th was no doubt my most liberating project up to that point. Although I was completely happy with each of my prior albums, something about them felt incomplete. I did not feel free to speak to certain more controversial topics that were dear to my heart. I felt that I was expected to chastise the Black community about fatherlessness and high rates of crime but remain silent about the racial injustices that create cycles of poverty and violence.

Looking back now, I realize that I was ensnared by what I call "the evangelical edit." I was constantly bumping up against walls and expectations—some overt, some invisible—that sought to shift my story from truth for the sake of others' comfort. I was encouraged to entertain youth groups with hip-hop music and culture, but I was not allowed to call them out on cultural insensitivity. Even in Black churches, I felt the edit. Many churches employed me to engage their youth and young adults while levying ridiculous restrictions that left me feeling like a parody of myself.

This album was a rebirth for me, both as an artist and as an individual. I felt that I had gained my creative independence—that I didn't have to create music solely for the consumption of youth groups. And with that freedom came the realization that we self-edit when we feel we are inferior. We hold ourselves back because we're afraid that if we don't, others will. We stop ourselves from living our full creative life, from telling the stories we were created to tell.

The album was both revered and reviled. One publication gushed about aspects of the record ("challenging, rough, raw, provoking, and stirring"), then turned and immediately dismissed it as being "written exclusively to African-Americans."[12] Although the critic ended his review with praise, that implied narrative haunted me. My previous albums, which reference many White theologians and historical figures, were albums for everyone. What made the difference here? My new reticence to edit myself under the dishonest story demanded by the White gaze? After all, is it only Black people who need to learn Black history?

It is our freedom that is at stake here. It is our ability to participate in the making of a better world, in the seeking of justice and restoration. And often it is our faith that's at stake too. I've had many friends abandon their Christian faith because of dishonest or dangerous narratives. This matters.

We are not lacking in bad theology or incomplete stories. I don't believe we need a new Christianity, but I think we need *true* Christianity. A Christianity with honesty and dignity. A Christianity that embraces the gold and the shadow of its history. That tells the right story and, rather than pushing us to hold ourselves back, can set us free to unleash our creative gifting, no matter what that gifting is. A Christianity that helps us recover the story of our Creator—and the image in which we were made.

I hope for us to find the *goodness* of God despite false narratives that exploit or restrict us. The Bible is a good story, told honestly. God cares about how we tell stories and how those stories shape the world. A good story benefits all. A good story tells the truth without partiality. A good story is honest and sees the value in others.

The world we live in is a mosaic of our collective imagination. We build it together, one word, one hour, one song or painting or sermon or meal at a time. Will we let this place be shaped by bad dreamers? Will we choose the colors of liberation or limitation?

Let's hear that ancient wind of affirmation—*he saw that it was good.* Let's allow it to guide us through the toughest times when even dignity seems to have deserted us. In that image is our identity.

Oh, and let me be the first to say it.

You look good in red.

2

GOOD CALL

> Mostly, people are made poor by the actions of others—directly or indirectly. Poverty is caused. And the primary cause is the exploitation of others by those whose own selfish interests are served by keeping others poor.
>
> —CHRISTOPHER J. H. WRIGHT,
> *Old Testament Ethics for the People of God*

When my daughter was very young, she gazed up into my brown eyes and said, "Daddy, when I grow up, I want to work at Waffle House."

I had only one response to that self-revelation from my prudent, beautiful girl—to cry tears of joy. I immediately began to think of all the *free waffles* that I could one day get from my daughter. (Excuse me, but if you don't love Waffle House, then you might just be what's wrong with the world.)

Now seriously—of course I don't want my daughter to see a Waffle House career as the ultimate goal for her life.

But neither do I want her to feel less dignified if she doesn't find a career that perfectly fits the American dream. What do I want for her? What I want for all of us—to love the idea of working (and creating), to pursue what brings her joy. At that moment? It was waffles. Hallelujah.

And this little remembrance points to a vital truth. When it comes to our calling, the rules of good work, of meaning and creativity, aren't what we've been told they are.

We live in a world where work means trying to find the balance between provision and dignity. The 2020 pandemic has proven that many industries we thought were fail-proof can definitely do just that. From my perspective, only pride, indolence, or ignorance would keep us from working any job necessary in order to provide for ourselves and our loved ones. But beyond that baseline, we ought to ask, What is good work? What does it mean to bring creativity into our calling? What are the stories—true or false—that our culture tells us about work? And how can we bring what we do every day—no matter how humble—into the story of creation and redemption that God is writing so we can join him in healing this broken world?

To begin, it is important that we cleanse the stench off the word *work*. We've all encountered the common cultural stories of work either as endless, meaningless drudgery or as the whole purpose of human life. But work has an ominous shadow over it even in many Christian spaces. Often it seems like the importance of work is omitted because of a fixation on personal piety. After all, how can work be spiritual?

Sometimes work is even vilified because of an incomplete theology that teaches that it's a curse—a consequence of the Fall. We misread the story in Genesis, and before you know it, we're believing that labor is punishment. Of course, that isn't true. God's invitation to Adam (yes, right after he saw that it was good) was to name things and tend the garden. God blessed the first couple, telling them to be fruitful and multiply. Good work was never about the curse. It was never the result of sin. The institution of work was established because of the need to produce good things from the benevolent soil of Eden. Only after the Fall did our work retreat into shadow.

When I speak of work, I want to return to that original idea. Work, in that good sense, is simply human activity that produces results. Something is made. Something is done. This definition includes the artist who creates, the teacher who instructs, the parent who raises children, and the altruist who volunteers. It is not about payment or job descriptions.*

Whether or not work has always been *arduous* is a debate for another time. But work has always been *virtuous*. I believe much of our trouble today comes from a simple fact: we have lost the virtue we were meant to find in our vocations.

Tomorrow many of us will wake up loathing the thought

---

* I will often use the words *creation* and *calling* as proxies for the word *work*. I recognize that these words have some distinct differences. However, I also know that our society uses these terms loosely.

of our jobs. We will move through our morning prep with weighted feet. We will rehearse responses to expected confrontations and disappointments. *I wish someone would say something to test me today! I'll give them a piece of my mind.* As the workday draws closer, the clock will mock our reluctance. *It's time . . . it's time . . .*

Our narrative about work is passed down to us. If we feel negatively about vocation, we probably caught that perspective from our parents as they complained their way through their own career path (or lack of a path). We can probably find the same attitude in our children when we attempt to wake them in the morning. I know that many mornings I require biblical amounts of prayer and fasting to maintain sanity while waking my children from their slumber. (I have reason to believe it was easier for Jesus to raise Lazarus from the grave than it is to command an able-bodied teen to rise up from his or her bed and walk.) Interesting, isn't it, that these same children have no problem racing the sun when their day's itinerary is filled with activities they love?

In any case, many of us carry a plague—we don't believe that our work matters. And it kills something inside us. Why? Because we were made to participate in creating solutions and not just to work aimlessly.

Sin left nothing uncorrupted. When we disdain activities that don't immediately satisfy us, we are living into the essence of human brokenness. Whoever said that we could expect constant satisfaction? A theology that promises that is broken. Nevertheless, we find ourselves feeling like extras on the set of life, trying desperately to write a meaningful part for ourselves.

But, of course, we've already been given a good role. One that requires us to act out the image of God as we find our place in his story and to give of ourselves to make this world a little less broken. What if, instead of coping and complaining, we chose to believe this? To believe that we have a part to play—no matter how humble our role seems on the surface? What if we found the bravery to faithfully create in response to our calling, no matter how humble that calling is? What if we embraced the daily opportunities we are given to invest our time and our talent in our work?

God is good. And one of the implications of being made in his image is that we were made to cultivate good (*towb*[1]). We were made to work—not for mindless profit but for the benefit of the good world. To contribute to the welfare of creation. God (though omniscient) had no intention of releasing human greed and vanity into the workplace of the world. The exploitation and dead-end degradation of so much of our work today is the opposite of what God wanted for his images.

And guess what I'm going to say? That's right—*the story matters*. When we are discontented, what we produce will reflect our condition. And is that any way to create? No! We'd paint with less passion. We'd educate with less patience. We'd build with less care, less scrutiny.

We have to stop living from this smallness, this despair. Brokenness in society reproduces itself when we create from an identity smaller than the one God gave us, instead of reclaiming our rightful story.

When we reclaim that truer story, our creativity and calling can bring us the richness of contentment. In his brilliant piece "The Contented Man," G. K. Chesterton wrote,

> "Content" ought to mean in English, as it does in French, being pleased; placidly, perhaps, but still positively pleased. . . . Being content with an attic ought not to mean being unable to move from it and resigned to living in it. It ought to mean appreciating what there is to appreciate in such a position.[2]

Chesterton saw value in the attic's unique qualities instead of comparing it with, say, a palace. The attic is no different from many of our vocations. Contentment ignites the observation that all things have intrinsic value by simply being what they are.

And here's what happens when we really get that: contentment removes the obstructions that keep us from seeing properly. We see things as they are—ourselves, our work, and *God*. There is no true worship without contentment.

I remember hearing a quote that captures the heart of contentment: "If God has called you to be a trashman, don't stoop so low as to be a king."

Once, as I was returning to America from South Africa, I made a restroom stop in the Johannesburg airport. As I entered the restroom, a young gentleman working as the restroom attendant greeted me: "Welcome to my office."

Uh, okay. I gave him the obligatory smile and walked past him, thinking, *Calm down, brother. It's a restroom.* When I left, he maintained the same charisma and offered the same courtesy. I gave him the rand I had left over by way of a tip. But as I walked away, I couldn't shake something about the short encounter. As I began to process, I realized that I felt strange about the difference in our attitudes.

When I walked in, I had seen his work—attendant in an airport restroom—as nothing to hold in high honor. But he had held it in the highest honor. He welcomed me with pleasure to his place of service. (I might add that the restroom was spotless! Amazing, since as we know, filthy restrooms are one of the greatest consequences of the Fall.)

When you have a high regard for your work, you can change the climate around yourself. Whoever or whatever this gentleman worshipped—Jehovah, Allah, Unkulunkulu, or money—the story he believed about himself informed how he worked. This was a man who believed that even an airport restroom can be a place to produce *good* work. Through his dignity, he elevated the restroom to the status of his "office."

God is preeminent over prestigious positions as well as the "restrooms" we manage. Whether we work in a palace or a lion's den, God provides opportunities for us to reflect his character in our calling so that his glory may be centered. We are limited not by what we do but by how we do it.

Creativity can be a lot like worship. So can work. We can manipulate our creativity just like we can misdirect our worship. To work is in itself a benefit of being created in the image of God. After all, he works too. But what we do flows from what we believe. Our work and art directly reflect the type of God we believe in.

When worship is the posture from which we work, every detail and person in the world becomes important. When our creativity is grounded in worship, we become deeply content. Our contributions are not about prestige or production. They are about faithfulness.

The attic or restroom that serves as our office may not be as high a call as we want (it's okay to have ambition and want to expand our horizons), but it's a call we can see as holy. The more honor we bestow on even these humble positions, the more our dignity is affirmed. After all, it's difficult to see our dignity when we don't see our work in the world as dignified!

Even in the most undignified or exploitative settings, there were people who used their God-given creativity to reclaim their human dignity. We need to look no further than American slaves singing spirituals on the horrid plantations or chain gangs using crafty cadences to remind them of their humanity. The melody of the soul silences the mockery of our surroundings. Music, like all art, is the memory of virtue. No matter our setting, with imagination we can dignify it. Remake this broken world, even just a little.

Find freedom, even by the stalls of an airport restroom.

In 1968, sanitation workers in Memphis, Tennessee, went on strike. They hoped the city would recognize them as a union, providing them with much-needed improvement to their working conditions, including better equipment, merit-based promotions, and fair compensation.

The goal of these 1,300 workers was to convince the city of their reasonable demands and effect real change. These were men whose coworkers had been killed by the mechanical failures of dysfunctional garbage trucks. Many workers of color had been overlooked for promotion in favor of White coworkers. But the city didn't listen. So they filled the streets. Carrying signs that read "I am a man," they marched in rebuke to the city council and Henry Loeb, the mayor. It was an act of self-affirmation, of dignity.

Sometimes we need to remind ourselves of who we are. This is especially true when we're confronting challenges. The humanity of that message—"I am a man"—inspires me. To view our work as worship is not easy. But it begins with us affirming our humanity. We have been made in God's image.

We have many reasons to complain about our labor. Work is *work.* However, worship is not restricted to churches or cathedrals. If we believe God is sovereign, then we must believe that what he has made has a good purpose. We must see *good* not solely as what is good for me but as what is good according to the narrative of God. Within the narrative of God, neither our talents nor our work has ever been limited to what pleases us. Work can be for provision. Work can be for pleasure. Work can also be for purpose—*redemptive* purpose. Good work helps repair the damage done when humans decided to swerve God as the preeminent architect of all creation. It reinforces the true story.

When Christians theorize about the implications of Adam and Eve's disobedience, we often focus on death or the doctrine of personal damnation. Their disobedience started a war for the human heart. Now, as we saw in the previous chapter, our creativity can be all mixed up with false narratives about our work and can be hijacked to promote the most vile behaviors and beliefs.

We can lose ourselves. When that happens, our work breaks down. We become short-sighted. We educate with less patience. We build with less care. We tell dishonest stories.

In the beginning of the Bible's story, humanity was content. We were in perfect communion with God. Worship was not something we thought of as separate from the rest of life—it was intrinsic to our identity. Who we were. But because of sin, we who once reflected God's glory now try to steal it. We no longer find value in being subordinate to the Creator, but in a paradox of pride, we become subordinate to created things (Romans 1:25).

We humans were once unified in perfect community, but now we seek to exploit one another for personal gratification. We were given talents and the resources of a lavish garden to use for charitable purposes, only to use those talents and resources to extend greed and destruction. What we see now is an inversion in the whole physical and spiritual ecosystem of creation. We who once found purpose in our Creator now crave approval from the created. We no longer ask "What is God's intention for me?" but ask "What is *my* intention for me?"

Human history since the Fall has been the time line of a futile journey toward self-discovery while ignoring God's wise instructions. But praise be to God—there is a redeemer and restorer for those who acknowledge that they've been on a path to destruction.

Jesus removes our idolatry of self and restores our identity as the children of a faultless maker. *Saul saw that it was good on the road to Damascus.*

Jesus removes the corrupted intentions within our relationships and restores the hospitality in our communities. *The woman at the well saw that it was good when a Jewish man asked her for water.*

Jesus removes the selfishness in our labor and restores the generosity in our cultivation. *Zacchaeus saw that it was good from halfway up a sycamore tree.*

Jesus's death on the cross was both selfless and satisfying. Hebrews 10:14 states that "by one sacrifice he has made perfect forever those who are being made holy."[3] We are clay. But we who were once vessels of wrath are now being transformed into vessels of mercy. This transformation isn't just of the soul. It includes all of us. Jesus is redeeming our comprehensive being, everyday activities and all. Who we are *and* what we do. This redemption is both cognitive and corporeal. We aren't welcomed into a bodiless gospel. And we make from how we are being remade.

Yes, humanity is still plagued with a desire to disobey God. We know this to be true in our lives and in the lives of others. Humans are sinful, and sinful people *can* participate in sinful work. We must also recognize that our sinful work can reinforce complex networks—institutions and ideologies. These can produce policies and systems that perpetuate injustice, benefit some at the expense of others, and tell manipulative stories.

But the narrative of God's work doesn't end with human sin or systemic injustice. The gospel plays a role in the redemption of our corrupted work. We can have hope in our ability to cultivate this world. If Jesus is redeeming all things, is he not asking for our work to be informed by the good news of his gospel?

Like a lot of American theology, we can emphasize one doctrine at the expense of another. More conservative theologies do a good job remembering that our human nature has been corrupted. But when this becomes a cognitive gospel that is separated from the corporeal, we begin to make concessions to a "spiritual" life that emphasizes Bible study and personal piety while ignoring the fact that our work can be selfish. On the other side of things, a corporeal gospel separated from the cognitive is often subject to whimsical cultural presentations of good and evil.

The truth holds space for all of us. Jesus spoke about and lived a life that covered soul *and* body. Nothing is left out. How we work will testify to the type of God we believe in. If your work is concerned only with wealth or upward mobility and not the well-being of others, then your God has become a slumlord.

Work is not agnostic. Calling is spiritual. Every swing of a hammer is informed by an idea.

In the Old Testament, a couple of words are translated "called." *Za`aq* means "to call for help." Israel called out to the Lord for help (Exodus 2:23; Judges 3:9; Psalm 107:13). The other, *qara'*, is often used in the context of assigning a name to someone or something. It can also refer to God calling his children to help with a mission, such as when he chose Moses, Joshua, and Samuel.

In Exodus 31, the Lord *called* Bezalel to carry out a mission. One translation states that God had "specifically chosen" Bezalel.[4] The Lord filled him with the Spirit; therefore, he would have the ability and intelligence to complete the task. Bezalel's duty was to execute God's creative direction. Bezalel and others were tasked with the artistic design and furnishing of Israel's sacred gathering place. This assignment would bless God and their community. The Lord calls individuals to meet a need and fills them with the Spirit. He gives them wisdom—and everything else they need.

During the Exodus, when Moses addressed the people at Mount Sinai, he called them to the collective work of communal progress. Everyone, no matter how humble, had a part to play in Israel's exit from captivity and movement toward the Promised Land. They had a common call and met it as talent and opportunity allowed. I think of the 1963 March on Washington. It is easy for us to reduce the march to a singular moment in which Dr. Martin Luther King Jr. gave a riveting speech. However, the march was more than King's contribution. Americans must also thank A. Philip Randolph for proposing the idea of a march on Washington decades before the Southern Christian Leadership Conference executed theirs. The marchers were blessed by the angelic vocals of Mahalia Jackson. Tenacious organizers and charismatic celebrities were directly responsible for the famed gathering. Everyone had a part to play. We may remember only Moses during the Exodus or King during the march, but they stood in solidarity with a whole community that had been *called* to a larger purpose.

Just as he did with the March on Washington, the Lord called a diversity of people to contribute to the actions that were to take place once Moses descended from Sinai (Exodus 31; 35). Taxes were paid that contributed to the building of the tabernacle. Individuals gave to the work as they felt moved.

In the New Testament, two of the words translated "called" are *epilegō* ("to choose, to name") and *klētos* ("invited or appointed"). We are being invited into a mission where there is great need. Paul was called to a service he never asked for. He was promised suffering, not reward. This stands in contrast to our contemporary ideas about calling.

Our ideas about calling are often inspiring and poetic, but they can also be quite elitist and self-serving. Many people choose vocations out of the necessity to provide instead of choosing the career they really want. Very seldom in the Bible did people have the luxury of doing what they wanted. Many were called by God to fulfill a need. At times during this calling, the individual felt underqualified. This did not stop God from assigning him or her to the task. If anything, recognition of limitations makes a person more qualified for the job because of his or her dependence on God. Therefore, is it possible that our theology around calling should emphasize need over desire?

If you are an employee, you are given an assignment by your boss. You may not fully understand the assignment. However (ideally), your authorities have truly thought it through. There is a reason for the task assigned to you.

And here's the point—someone's vision is in play. In this sense, working can be very similar to another way we quietly shape the world—voting. As the book *Compassion (&) Conviction* states, "If we're not applying our values to our advocacy and voting, then we're applying someone else's."[5] When voting, we should know why we're casting our vote a particular way. There should be a larger picture.

When we work, we should have conviction behind every swing of the hammer—even if that conviction is as simple as faithfulness to the call Christ has given to help remake the world. As Christians, we should never leave our convictions at the church house once we are blessed with the benediction. Those convictions follow us home, maneuver with us through traffic, and wash us with courage as we enter our cubicles or construction zones. If we don't swing the hammer within the framework of our own convictions, then we swing it for the convictions of another. Are we creating with God's good vision in mind? Is our work building the kind of world that we see in the love and life of Jesus?

Psalm 19 speaks about creation proclaiming the glory of God.[6] Romans 1 states that creation's simple existence removes any excuse that people may have about not knowing their grand architect.[7] Psalm 19 says that this world speaks "without a sound or word."[8] This is a poetic statement of a poignant truth. God's creation can't help but tell the truth about God. It demonstrates his power. It publishes his glory.

Much of our work is done in quiet quarters. But just like God's work, it is far from silent. It speaks volumes as it preaches the intended message of its creator. What is your creation saying about *you*?

Whatever the specifics of our art and work, creativity is about reimagining the world. Often this looks like solving problems. Our work forces us to find new ways to provide for human needs. Work, like art, has many purposes, but one of its defining qualities is its innovative potential.

The '68 Memphis sanitation workers were providing a service that was solving a problem in the city. The mayor during that time wanted the service, but he didn't want to honor their work with dignity, shown by fair pay and the recognition of a union. Theirs was a job of high importance, but they weren't valued.

It's easy to dismiss sanitation work as just collecting garbage. But let's think about how many ramifications there are if a city doesn't handle its trash. Garbage will collect on street corners. The waste will increase the risk of pests spreading disease. A lack of sanitation puts higher pressure on health-care professionals. The city begins to lose its aesthetic appeal. As a consequence, the dirty city brings in less business. This diminishes the community's value, and people don't take ownership of where they live. The citizens begin to care less about their neighborhoods and schools. They invest less. And the cycle continues.

Sanitation work affects the economy and quality of life of the whole city. Whether or not we desire such work is irrelevant. Devaluing virtuous work is to say that God is not present in that activity. That is an evil philosophy. A demonic theology. The ability to solve problems is a direct reflection of our connection to God, our Creator. That is a creative life.

Many Christians teach that hell is an eternal destination without the presence of God. A place void of hope, creativity, love, joy, laughter, compassion, and care. I don't believe any human can fathom an earthly social condition that is tantamount to hell. Although some of us face unimaginable isolation and suffering, there is always the presence of hope before us. Hell is the worst condition possible—without the presence of *any* hope. No innovation. No activity that could be cathartic.

On earth, even the poorest laborer in the poorest country can find some dignity or joy in creating. Creating can be therapy in itself. The act of creating can provide new resources. No matter our earthly circumstances, there is always an attribute of God that cuts through the darkness.

However, we willingly promote hell in our daily practice. Many people carry a dangerous dualism into their Mondays that silences their religious belief. I'm not speaking of the lack of preaching, Bible studies, or evangelism in the workplace. I'm speaking of sending people into the world equipped with a theology that is sufficient only for Sundays. These are ambassadors leaving embassies with the commission to rebuild and redeem societies but without the tools or instructions to do so. When we keep God out of our work, we are working in hell.

In 2007, I spent over two weeks in Jayapura, Papua, teaching a cohort of artists how to use their art for education and spiritual formation. While this was certainly far from hell, some of the artists did live in significant material poverty. But during that time, I saw that there was no way their poverty would bankrupt their creativity. Their imagination was all the currency they needed. I was inspired.

We set up speakers and microphones on an open plot of land. The canvas was set for us (the native artists and the westerners with me) to share an image of God that was generally unknown to this mostly Muslim territory. My initial intention had been to use the stage as an altar—to proselytize the unbelieving crowd. But I quickly saw that what was needed was to simply heed the call to worship, without focusing on the outcome. I learned in that experience that art could be a temple for others to witness God's attributes through us. That it could be simple. Of course, I still believe that "the end of the matter . . . [is to] fear God and keep his commandments,"[9] but if our worship can't include a good backspin and freestyle, then I don't know whether that faith is worth my time. God is with us in the temple of our art as we release our gifting and creativity to him in simple work and praise.

Why do we work? If we want to change our society, the answer to that question must be found outside ourselves. Does my work benefit others or just my own interests? Like my daughter's aspiration for a career at Waffle House, when children talk about their future vocations, they are often full of joy. But somewhere between adolescence and adulthood, there is a shift from purity to prosperity.

Most of our language around work relates to profit and provision. Those are good, of course, but if they're all we see, then we fail to emphasize the reward of serving others through our careers. Kids who start out wanting to be doctors because it's fun and helpful become adults who can only see the income. As kids inch closer to adulthood, we impress on them the need to go to college. Sure, college might teach them how to make a living. But are we teaching them how to make a *life*? When work is about *making a living,* we turn a blind eye to what doesn't benefit our bottom line. But *making a life* sees the whole picture—including how others could be pushed to the margins as an effect of our success.

To understand the gold and shadow of our cultivating, we must think not only of what is overtly egregious. Sin and evil work through more than the vile, violent, and ugly. Sin and evil are parasites attached to any condition that denies humans the capacity to experience the presence of God. What does this mean? That while work is inherently good, not every job is.

Some work—in a horrible parody of its divine intention—is exploitative and evil. If we were having a casual Wednesday Bible study and in walked a pimp with a group of prostitutes, many Christians would judge them for their cursed work. The saints would assume that these individuals had never tasted the waters of a saving faith. Not only would they attempt to teach them of a grace that corrects and forgives, but they would also encourage a new vocation.

Now, the church would be right to want justice, even to call them out. This work devalues the humanity of these women—as a commodity to be bought—and gives an improper, exploitative authority to the pimp. It's an example of the inverted ecosystem established after the Fall.

But let's imagine this same Bible study again. Now a payday-loan lender enters the room. This man spends his days lending small sums at exorbitant interest, taking advantage of the undereducated and down-on-their-luck. But would he receive the same backlash as the pimp? I'm not so sure. Not only might reproof be withheld, but he might even be asked to speak on stewardship and leadership if his business is successful.

Why do we have this hypocrisy or selective sight about the impact of evil work on our communities? Maybe it's because we've never had it pointed out. Maybe it's because we've believed wrong stories about success. Or maybe, just maybe, we find it difficult to see ourselves as the ones perpetrating injustice. We want to think we are the heroes. We want to think we would have been Harriet Tubman or Anne Frank. We don't want to see ourselves as complicit in or blind to evil.

But if we want to see where our ethics would have landed us in tumultuous historical times, all we have to do is see what we practice when there is peace. Where you would have landed in the story is based on your surroundings, your circumstances, and what stories formed your identity. Evil is not accidental. Nor is heroism. People don't wake up heroes; they decide to participate in daily practices that push them toward heroism.

And this daily formation is why calling is so important. Our work is daily, and it daily forms us. We have to do exactly what this whole chapter has been about—find a better understanding of our calling. What does it mean that God has called *you*? Many of us believe without question that pastors and missionaries are called to their vocations. But can you say with conviction that you've been called to your role? I hope so. My brother Dhati has been called to pastor a church. My friend Paul has been called to be a traffic engineer, managing the city's transportation infrastructure. Both of these vocations can reveal creative gold. Both can form these beloved men. Both can be part of reimagining this world.

No matter what it is, your work can be meaningful. Our work is spiritual because of how we work, not where we work. All work has spiritual importance. We are called. That is what matters.

We often use "being called" as a spiritual way to justify our discontentment. But we can't use calling to escape from our commitments. Instead, we should try to see them as God does. As long as the conversation is centered on upward mobility, we cannot see the dignity of where we are. The success of a calling will be measured by the amount of pleasure a person receives from it. We will also teach people it's acceptable to ignore their needs and chase every fleeting desire.

Here are some important questions to ask ourselves: *Why has God placed me here at this time? What is the redemptive goal of my work? Am I working for the glory of God or the glorious dollar?*

God demonstrated the power of work and cultivation in Genesis. He hovered over the void and created beauty and meaning. As humans made in God's image, we have the ability to wake up every morning and create beauty and meaning too. Each morning is empty and without form. There is no narrative yet. We hover over the emptiness and make decisions to create.

Will what we make be good?

WHERE IS PRUDENCE?

The jungle was a congress of noise.

However, if the creatures had still cared enough to listen, they might have discerned the difference between courtesy and noise. They might have remembered that there had been a time when there was balance in the golden shadows of the palms and harmony between the voices of all animals. They might have remembered what they were there for.

But they had grown arrogant and shrill, until they had forgotten that there was ever another way. As the days recycled, the beasts of the jungle thirsted for validation. They prayed and sang for it, danced for it, worked and died for it. They forgot themselves. And in that, they slowly descended.

By the time they looked to the sky, it was too late. Angelic judgment hovered above. They could not mount a defense. There was nowhere to retreat. This arrival was unannounced. They would learn to listen again. Or they would die.

The sky itself was insignificant. What was important were the invaders who occupied it. Wings over wings. Wheels in horrible wheels. Eyes everywhere. The spectators wanted to flee, but curiosity held them there. They had heard tales of strange creatures before but had mocked the legends. Now the legends had come. These winged invaders looked like none of the winged friends they could name. The jungle did not know their name, but their purpose was greater than any name the jungle could give them.

It might have been different if the invaders had been beautiful. Perhaps the creatures would have welcomed them as guests. They loved beautiful things. It was much easier to listen to beautiful things. But though they were majestic, these were not beautiful guests. Invaders are never beautiful.

The foreigners descended. Their wings split the air, and the observers' insecurity grew. The invaders formed a court of judgment above their heads. On the ground, fearful whispers turned to silence.

"Gather your commissioners, the council who oversees your politics, pleasure, and stories. There is much learning to be done," spoke a winged stranger.

"Who might we say is requesting their presence?" one creature asked. No answer came. Trembling, the beast ran to obey.

The court's eyes surveyed the animals. They felt strangely guilty. Finally their leaders arrived, displaying a veneer of confidence and piety but quailing under the judging gaze.

"Who placed the veil over the land?" the invader asked them. "Who thought it wise to veer from the design?" His strange eyes narrowed. "Since the beginning, Prudence has lived among you. She watched over you. She brought civility and balance. Where is Prudence now?"

The leaders of the land crouched before these unexpected judges. The winged magistrate stated, "Prudence has been gone for some time, and you have not taken heed. Was she killed?" There was a dramatic pause, but the invaders expected no answer. "Did she depart and leave you to your decadence?" The court fell silent again. "Now your ecosystem is disturbed. You are too proud to acknowledge her absence as a judgment."

Each sentence was more ominous than the last. There was no defense for the council. Their prestige could not defend them. Their prayers were simple, their songs were reckless, their dancing was vain, their work was mercenary, and they would die soon.

The words of the hovering magistrate echoed. "She was essential to this ecosystem that has been tempted by depravity, and there were no songbirds to minister to her. You were too consumed by your progress and pleasures to hear her trills. Now you will be consumed with a trill from heaven."

The invaders spread their wings with a cry. Pure darkness poured from them, and the sky darkened to a disturbing shade.

"Be gracious to us!" cried the jungle creatures.

"Bring forth your council!" said the invaders.

There was no hesitation. A council of six stepped forward. This was the worst time to have influence.

The first member of the council slowly emerged from the group: a pedantic primate of high repute.

The primate spoke with proud eloquence. "Salutations. I am innocent in this matter, and probably we all are. I am not a violent beast. I would not harm a beetle, let alone the winged Prudence. And note our accomplishments! We are advancing as students of the soil. We are more learned than ever before. Why would we need to be watched? And by a failure, no less! The presence of this so-called Prudence has been inconvenient and has done little to remove intolerance and dogmatism. If death befell our demure friend, then it is the fault of her commitment to old manners and dying customs."

A member of the high court looked upon the primate. "Your arrogance led you to speak first. Ill-advised. True, you are not violent with your limbs, but you are violent with your words. What you think is progress is a descent. You are never satisfied. You *claim* concern for those on the margins of the land, but you have no true interest in their well-being. Those in need have looked to you. You've failed them. Of course Prudence's presence would inconvenience you. The ecosystem is unbalanced because of your arrogance. You've removed a root that nourished you all. Let that be a judgment."

"We tolerate your folly no longer," sang the whole chorus of those above the beasts. A whoop rang out from them. The sky darkened even more. The fear in the primate's eyes brought concern to the audience.

The second member of the council slowly slithered before the rest: a rebellious, revolutionary reptile known for his persuasion.

He spoke with slick eloquence. "I salute you, honorable visitors. Forgive our jungle for its corruption. I've tried to reason with the perpetrators and cleanse this place of its foul stench. Prudence asked for my assistance, but I was busy campaigning. There are many here that can vouch for me. Prudence sought me at the wrong time. If the strange creature Prudence has been harmed, then she must have been the agitator. If she has left, maybe she hated our little democracy. We've debated, convened, revolted, and voted. If something's wrong, it's not us. It's the fault of archaic ideas."

A member of the high court looked at the reptile. "You ignored Prudence. You avoided her request because it brought judgment on you. You lobbied for approval. She earned it without campaigning. You blame the victim. Her wisdom does not age, and yours is fleeting."

"We entertain your swindling no longer," sang the lofty winged foreigners.

The invaders spread their wings. The fear in the reptile's eyes brought further concern to the audience as the sky darkened even more.

The third member of the council scurried before the rest: an affluent rodent known for her productivity.

The rodent spoke rapidly. "Acknowledgments, revered judges. We are in the process of great renewal. So excuse what might be unpleasant to your eyes. We are growing. We are moving. We are building a future. If I had known our prudent friend was unwelcome or in danger, I would have assisted her myself. Investigate my reputation! I have means. I have been charitable. What guilt do I have in this matter? I can only humbly suggest that the coy creature did not toil hard enough. I have no greater prize than that of my labor. While Prudence watched over us, she surely could have worked with us."

A member of the high court looked upon the rodent. "Your opulence and industry are empty. What you think are pathways are obstructions. Your busyness never impressed the prudent watcher. You envied her modesty. You couldn't buy her friendship. Your 'charity' is bribery. You tore down her home for your advancement. You can't build dignity. Your once-noble work has become avarice."

"You will no longer negotiate here," sang those in the sky. Again wings beat, a whoop rang out, and the heavens darkened.

The fourth member of the council strutted before the rest: a mesmerizing peacock known for his allure.

His speech employed theatrics. "Holy hosts! Admired arbitrators! We would have prepared a grand reception if we had been notified of your visitation. However, there are no better guests to have interrupt our festivities. I must communicate my deep condolences for Prudence's loss. Our friend deserves a proper eulogy—which we'll give, of course. The land must know of the void left by her absence! I only wish she would have shown more affability and courtesy. She was stiff, you know. Rude. Didn't think much of my feathers. Really, without taste, what was the point of her, anyway?"

"Your tongue speaks well," a magistrate replied, "but you reek of malevolence. You care only for grand receptions and proper eulogies so your obnoxious plumage can be on full display. You had many in your presence who were worth attention, but you stole their glory. Your beauty was once liberating, but now it has become a distraction. You are pleasant on the eyes, yet you envied Prudence for her flight and freedom to wander without creating a spectacle."

"You will find no admirers here," the magistrates

sang. The fear in the peacock's eyes brought greater concern to the audience, and the atmosphere darkened yet again.

The fifth member of the council stepped forward: a jejune sheep known for her hospitality.

She spoke with wavering confusion. "It's not our *fault*, you know. We have no slick tongue nor any high argument. We acknowledge the purity before us. If you find guilt in us, it's not from following our own intuition. We have been misled! Prudence didn't lead us! If she had done something, we would have listened. It's not our *fault*."

"Your disposition is almost fitting," said one of the winged strangers. "But your wavering is rooted not in conviction but in convenience. You've been herded in vogue. Judgment came upon you when you refused to acknowledge your responsibility. You believed ill things of Prudence, your friend and advocate. You blamed her for not speaking. But it is you who did not ask."

"You will gain conviction today," the chorus sang. Fear rushed through the jungle as the darkness deepened.

The sixth council seat was filled by a dole of birds who cautiously fluttered upward. The birds of the jungle were more pious than all. The chaplains of the flock began a song. They congregated in the air above the rest of the council like a low-hanging cirrus cloud.

The other creatures looked upon them in hope. Their presence was gentle. Their song was melodic. The dole's offering never ceased to amaze the onlookers of the jungle. Surely they would not fail to call mercy down from the surreal court who hovered above them.

But what was music to the beasts was shrill shriek-ing to those above. The words were clichés of empty piety, the melody discordant. With a swift swoop, an invader cut through the pious little flock like the sun cuts shadows.

"Your songs have not reached heaven, nor do they even bless the ground," shouted a flaming invader. "This will be your last song sung in dishonesty. You should have blessed that which you cursed, and you should have cursed that which you blessed. Your 'cleanliness' is sacrilege. You cry for grace and mercy. You ask where it is. It is right where you wanted it. You have been left to your own devices. You have no prayers, no songs, no dances, and nothing to work for. You only have an obligation to die."

And with that, the sky was quiet.

3

GOOD SLAVES, MAD PLANTATIONS

> When a people are subjected to such oppression,
> they are driven inward, to the depths of the very
> humanity the oppression is trying to negate. Any
> cultural expressions that emerge from such a
> suffering people will come from those human
> depths. . . . The skills to express such depth are
> what is today popularly known as "soul."
>
> —CARL F. ELLIS JR., *Free at Last?*

The leaves embraced strange colors in the early fall of 2014. The foundations of the oaks didn't seem as stable. Strong winds threatened them. The limbs were shifting to and fro. The harmonies sung by the birds sounded distressed. These were curious times.

The same antagonizing winds seemed to rush around my church, creating chaos and tension. Our spiritual temperature changed drastically. The blood rose in some and rushed out of others. Our claps had less reverb, and our songs lacked harmony. The sermons were muted, and the hospitality felt trite.

Why? Because on August 9, 2014, Michael Brown had been killed—murdered, many felt—by police officer Darren Wilson. And the wind could not blow that away.

We were a multicultural church with minority pastors. These were leaders who understood injustice from their own experience. We were the model of how to build a multiethnic space in a large city. Pastors and leaders had come from all over to learn our methods and philosophies. Quite a few even praised us for the very thing that has evaded many multicultural churches—our music. We gave popular contemporary Christian music a face-lift to appease our diverse community. (I like to call it "Chocolate Hillsong.") And, of course, it only made sense that such a cauldron would stir up a healthy dialogue. We'd had differences of opinion before. But this felt different.

Some sisters and brothers in my church chastised other sisters and brothers for their views on the shooting. There seemed to be irreconcilable differences between them. Others just wanted it all to go away—hoping the storm would pass and take the tension with it. Leaves were blowing in every direction. There was no harmony anymore, no clear way to gather what was being scattered.

The strong wind tipped us. During that time, relationships crumbled and philosophies fell. I remember thinking, *It was all good just a week ago. How could it unravel so quickly? We sat in the same pews and sang the same songs.*

An oak tree can look beautiful yet be hollow. I felt that our community was like that. Or maybe worse off—like a patient in need of a heart transplant but comfortable only with cosmetic surgery. We were close, but that didn't mean we were authentically connected. Maybe we were sitting just close enough to one another to discover how distant we were. An idol had been smashed and the implications were far reaching. Some felt liberated. Others were confused.

Our life experience shapes how we see theology, church engagement, and Jesus. What type of Jesus do you believe in? I like to borrow a question from Reggie Williams, author of *Bonhoeffer's Black Jesus:* "Was your Christ crucified?"[1]

The death of Michael Brown made us question our cultural theology. It was the catalyst for some of us to drop out of our common conversation while others reevaluated their education. Tragedy and trauma are like heat turned up under a pot of water. You can hold the lid down, but it *will* boil. You can suffocate a bubbling pot for only so long. The truth will rise. And it will always expose what is there, whether we are prepared for it or not.

The fall of 2014 impelled us to recalibrate what we believed. Who is Jesus, and what does he care about?

Our problem was that we were two churches who thought we were one. We used the same lyrics but sang different songs. We listened to the same words but heard different sermons. We drove down the same streets and lived in the same place, but maybe we had a different Christianity—though we both prayed to Jesus.

There was a Jesus for them, it felt like, and a Jesus for us.

But are there two Christs?

Our theology, just like our art and work, should try to make sense of our circumstances. This need is even more prevalent in minority communities. How have our stories and theology in America created two Christs? Because there has been one stream of Christian theology that benefits the powerful and one that liberates the oppressed. But as tempting as it is to feel that there are multiple Christs in circulation who are completely unrelated, I believe that the reality is a bit more nuanced—that the Christ of the Bible is fairly complicated.

We have trouble seeing Jesus in all his subtle nuance. Instead, we have created and consumed a falsely bifurcated Christ in our literature, music, and theology. Depending on our views and background, we can choose which of his teachings we like and which we'd prefer to ignore. My assessment is that Black Christian expression, especially in its art, has never departed from the Jesus of justice. He is a savior who cares about pain, liberation, and provision. This is why Black gospel music tends to love communal supplications for provision while contemporary Christian music popular among White majority culture tends to be more about what I might call "intrapersonal investigations of piety." Now, both are great spiritual disciplines that Christ affirms. Both are well intended and meant for good. But why do we have such trouble holding them together in holy tension?

In 1852, abolitionist Harriet Beecher Stowe released the fictional antislavery melodrama *Uncle Tom's Cabin*. Stowe finds herself in rare company as an author whose work reshaped her society. The book follows the life of Tom, a slave and a devoted Christian. His perseverance through injustice and peril is nothing short of otherworldly and is at times incomprehensible. Uncle Tom is more than an exceptional character. He is downright angelic.

Stowe's Uncle Tom was effective in evoking her readers' sympathy. The book became the bestselling novel of the nineteenth century, and Stowe's narrative challenged the indifference of many Northerners and the silent compliance of many Southerners.

Stowe's efforts were powerful, genuine, and an admirable form of advocacy. They were instrumental in swaying public opinion toward abolition. So it is rather unfortunate that today the name "Uncle Tom"—used as an epithet for Black capitulation to White oppression—is so far from her intentions. But however genuine her intentions and though *Uncle Tom's Cabin* was inspired by actual accounts, it's hard to imagine a human with Tom's level of heavenly resistance. No matter how bleak the plight that Tom finds himself in, how harsh the beatings, or how cruel the broken promises, he remains genial, compliant, and nonviolent. However, to be fair to Stowe, many of her characters were limited in their emotional range. (Tom becomes even more interesting when you compare his narrative with that of George, another slave who escapes to the North with his family and returns violence with violence.)

Despite the cultural impact of the book, Stowe received pertinent critiques from her abolitionist counterparts. William Lloyd Garrison, abolitionist, journalist, and social reformer, published strong critiques of Stowe's book in his newspaper, *The Liberator*. Garrison wrote,

> [Uncle Tom's] character is sketched with great power and rare religious perception. It triumphantly exemplifies the nature, tendency and results of Christian non-resistance. We are curious to know whether Mrs. Stowe is a believer in the duty of non-resistance for the white man. . . . Is there one law of submission and non-resistance for the black man, and another law of rebellion and conflict for the white man? When it is the whites who are trodden in the dust, does Christ justify them in taking up arms to vindicate their rights? And when it is the blacks who are thus treated, does Christ require them to be patient, harmless, long-suffering, and forgiving? And are there two Christs?[2]

What we witness in this exchange is not a far cry from what we find in our churches today. Garrison made a legitimate argument that can be posed to many Christians today. Is there a Christ who will "justify them taking up arms" to defend their liberties while the Christ of the marginalized "require[s] them to be patient, harmless, long-suffering, and forgiving"? This spiritual doublethink is often used to critique community rallies and marches but to support coups and political protests. This is the same theology that praised George Washington and Andrew Jackson while rebuking John Brown, Nat Turner, and Denmark Vesey. It is why, in the strange autumn of 2014, the very air of our church seemed unsettled.

I don't want to oversimplify a complex debate. But I have to ask the hard questions. What will our God have us believe about justice? How does our view of justice paint the attributes of God for those watching?

We must be careful not to construct a savior convenient for our personal interests or limited to our political binaries. False narratives and political strategies have divided Christian allegiances on both the progressive and the conservative sides. Again and again, the American church has traded Christian fidelity for cultural power. We seem less concerned with biblical principles than our political allegiance. Again—this is true of Christians on both sides of the political aisle. Why is faithfulness so hard?

I am told there is a Jesus who cares about the sanctity of life. But does that Jesus also care about the life of a human being when he is unarmed and gunned down by police officers? Does the Jesus who cares about police brutality also care about the unborn lives lost to abortion?

I am told there is a Jesus who urges us to address sex trafficking. But does that Jesus also care about the culturally acceptable pornography and music industries that fuel the demand for such a demoralizing reality?

I am told there is a Jesus who calls missionaries to developing countries. But does that Jesus also care about the imperialistic practices and colonial greed that created the poverty that requires humanitarian efforts and service projects in the first place?

As Christians, we do not have the luxury of assigning all evil to one ideology. As long as we identify evil by what our opposition believes, our God is subject to our personal politics. He is not Lord of lords; he is limited by legislation. We will always have two Christs.

Dr. Carl Ellis Jr. gave a charge to Christians who feel homeless in the political landscape: "I believe that if we are going to move forward as a community who has distinctive concerns in America, we need to evaluate political and social ideas as they stand on their own, without regard to their ideological association."[3]

This is a clarion call not just to marginalized Christians but to Christendom as a whole in this country.

We often lean toward theologies that fit neatly with our personal circumstances. This is true for all of us. But we must be aware of the limitations of those theologies. We must always have a posture of humility when it comes to the application of truth in the world. When the world is looking for a partisan parent in God, we must understand that we have a complex Father. This is not to say that there are no Christian positions. It is to affirm that we must be humble.

The ugly predicaments in life refine us, like pressure makes diamonds. Our experiences, filtered through our understanding of Jesus, determine how we perform our theology and live the creative life. If you grew up on a plantation, it is likely that you would develop plantation theology. I no longer expect someone completely disconnected from concerns of justice to see the crucified distinction in Jesus that Reggie Williams suggested.

Let's compare the theology of Black abolitionist David Walker, who lived in the early 1800s, with that of poet Phillis Wheatley, one of colonial America's great Black voices. Both of them believed slavery was inhumane and opposed to the character of God. They experienced oppression firsthand. However, they had different ideas about how to deal with the institution.

David Walker was a writer, entrepreneur, and Christian who never knew slavery but advocated for its immediate end. He grew in popularity by sharing pro-Black ideologies and horror stories of slavery in his pamphlet titled *Walker's Appeal*.

Walker was not one to shy away from conflict. His pamphlet was said to have created such a great upheaval among Southern slave owners that they offered a $3,000 bounty for Walker's death.[4] Walker did not allow the threats to deter him from his call to aid in the abolition of slavery. "I will stand my ground. *Somebody must die in this cause. I may be doomed to the stake and the fire, or to the scaffold tree, but it is not in me to falter if I can promote the work of emancipation."[5]

His indictment of American religion was just as radical as his physical bravery. Walker severely chastised those who misused God for their own wicked agendas. In his pamphlet, he left no doubt as to how he felt about using God's name as a justification for slavery:

Can any thing be a greater mockery of religion than the way in which it is conducted by the Americans? . . . They chain and handcuff us and our children and drive us around the country like brutes, and go into the house of the God of justice to return Him thanks for having aided him in their infernal cruelties inflicted upon us. . . . I call God . . . to witness, that your destruction is at hand, and will be speedily consummated unless you repent.[6]

Walker carried a theology of retribution that isn't often associated with Christian love. I believe Walker felt that the way to deal with the infection of a body part is to cut it off. This is loving the rest of the body rather than allowing the infection to spread. Slavery should have been seen as a gangrenous practice that forced Christians into action. However, many found themselves indifferent or complicit. This affected not only their theology but also the theology of others.

Then there was Phillis Wheatley. She was a prolific poet and faithful Christian who had been born in West Africa, then sold as a slave to Boston tailor John Wheatley and his wife, Susanna. John was an evangelical supporter of the preacher George Whitefield and his missionary work. Whitefield's death left a great impact on Phillis Wheatley. She wrote a poem eulogizing him in 1770, including powerful phrases such as these:

> Behold the prophet in his tow'ring flight!
> He leaves the earth for heav'n's unmeasur'd height.[7]

Whitefield was certainly a revered man of his day. However, even though "thy sermons in unequall'd accents flow'd, / And ev'ry bosom with devotion glow'd,"[8] he lobbied for slavery to continue. He was willing to preach a cognitive liberation to Africans but not a corporeal liberation. I believe Whitefield's fractured theology affected Phillis Wheatley. Her story was shaped by the one he told.

In June 1772, England's common law court ruled in favor of James Somerset, an escaped slave who had been recaptured and forced aboard a ship heading to Jamaica. This ruling weakened the grip of slavery in Britain. It essentially meant that any enslaved person that made it to England was free.

The following year, Wheatley toured England with her poetry. Many scholars find it hard to believe that Wheatley could travel London alongside antislavery advocates like Granville Sharp without knowing the possibility of becoming a free woman. Yet with all the opportunity before her to stay and be free, she decided to return to Boston to live with her owners.

That choice was not uncommon. Wheatley's literary friend Jupiter Hammon wrote about choosing to remain enslaved even if given the opportunity for freedom:

> Though for my own part I do not wish to be free, yet I should be glad if others, especially the young Negroes, were to be free; for many of us who are grown up slaves, and have always had masters to take care of us, should hardly know how to take care of ourselves; and it may be more for our own comfort to remain as we are.[9]

Although Wheatley was soon set free by her owners, her decision to return to Boston with them shows the psychological impact of oppression. Her identity had been shaped by the story she had been told about herself.

But the story doesn't end there. When she became a free woman, Phillis Wheatley used her pen more aggressively. In her letter to the widow of Revolutionary War general David Wooster, Wheatley offered solace to the grieving wife while praising the heroism of her dead husband. However, she slightly pivoted for a stanza to question the hypocrisy in colonial freedom fighting:

> But how, presumptuous shall we hope to find
> Divine acceptance with th'Almighty mind—
> While yet (O deed ungenerous!) they disgrace
> And hold in bondage Afric's blameless race?[10]

This is the same woman who eight years earlier, albeit under oppressive circumstances, lauded a man who lobbied in *support* of slavery!

What can we take from Wheatley's growth? First, we see that any thinking or creating under the watchful eye of an oppressor is likely to be censored and anemic. No matter how resolute Uncle Tom and Phillis Wheatley were in their acceptance of an enslaved state, we have to imagine that much of that was an act of self-preservation in an oppressive structure. Second, we see that people can evolve. Once liberated from oppression, we can harbor compassion and courage in the same vessel. Christianity doesn't make us docile and weak. It makes us earnest and resilient. It makes us able to hold tension—one can mourn the death of a colonial soldier while stating the flaws of the system his sacrifice upheld.

When our Jesus gets too small, our souls become stunted. The stories we tell change—and not for the better. When plantation owners did theology, their Christ became complicit in horrible things. Even when slaves in that system became Christians, their spirituality was complex. Their faith walked the fine line between submission and resistance. Between resolute forgiveness and the active pursuit of justice. Just as in Stowe's book I admire Tom's commitment to pacifism in the face of violence, I can also admire George's willingness to take up arms and defend his liberties and family as slave hunters attempted to seize him. This is honest storytelling—like the Christ who both wept *and* flipped tables.

In America, Black theology has its roots in the injustice of the plantation. Therefore, its primary roles were to defend the image of God and Black dignity, to restore people's view of God after the distorted theology of slave masters, and to reconstitute the Negro's place in America after emancipation. It's only right that the art and practices that proceeded from this theology would naturally speak to justice, redemption, and innovation.

Theology from the "big house" was different from theology in the field. While many White theologians had the luxury of spending hours pontificating about the intricacies of soteriology or other doctrines, Black thinkers and their White sympathizers were simply building basic arguments—that slaves were humans deserving of personal salvation and the inalienable right of freedom.

But from these roots, something incredible grew—a theology that yearns for liberation and compassion rather than power and autonomy. As plantation theology matured from a conflict theology to a more comprehensive theology, it began to grow into something more than simply a response to oppression. It took on its own beauty and character, confronting "the doctrine of demons" that had sneaked into pulpits across America.[11]

And all along, people were singing this theology, preaching it, writing it, painting it in folk art. They were *living* it, and it began to change them. And as they were changed, so was the world.

Early Black history in America is the story of resistance, perseverance, and defiant joy. Black art is the creative expression of those postures. In this way, the heritage of Black creativity offers lessons for anyone, regardless of background, who wants to connect joyful resistance to the persevering imagination.

Early on, Black creativity took the form of spirituals, songs from the fields that married the corporeal and the cognitive. The spiritual "Heav'n, Heav'n" is the epitome of a rich plantation theology that found the equilibrium of "on earth as it is in heaven":

I got shoes; you got shoes;
All of God's children got shoes.
When I get to heav'n, gonna put on my shoes.
I'm gonna walk all over God's heav'n, heav'n, heav'n.
Everybody talkin' 'bout heav'n ain't goin' there.

On the surface this song seems quite elementary. But it has a much deeper truth than God supplying his children's minor needs. This song is a strong rebuke to a slave-master theology that withheld basic human needs—like shoes—from slaves. *"I got shoes . . ."* Slaves were *denied* shoes and other necessities. The people who first sang these lines did so barefoot. These men and women were able to rejoice because they knew they served a God who cared about them, who would one day supply them with shoes. This song reaches for heaven while yearning for justice in the here and now.

And there is resistance too. When the singer proclaims, "Everybody talkin' 'bout heav'n ain't goin' there," it's a direct rebuke to slave masters who talked "heaven" but lived in total contradiction to the gospel.

Newfound post–Civil War citizenship didn't change the texture of the Negro Christian's belief. Freedom only gave more reason to write and sing about a merciful and just God. In order to survive the White supremacy that would manifest itself in the form of the Jim Crow, "separate but equal" South, the community needed a just and watching Lord, one taking notes on inequity.

And inequity there was—in plenty. Even setting aside the incredible structural efforts to keep Black people in "their place," racial stereotypes in so-called entertainment were prevalent. These ranged from the wildly popular minstrel shows discussed earlier to D. W. Griffith's landmark film *The Birth of a Nation,* which endorsed the Ku Klux Klan and portrayed free Black people as shiftless, barbaric, and oversexual. This film took the sensationalism of "White purity" and racial terror to the next level.

Plantation theology evolved, broadened. Spirituals faded as Black people moved from slavery to Reconstruction and into the long era of Jim Crow segregation. Each era deserved its own soundtrack and found it as jazz, blues, and early rock 'n' roll all grew out of a history of oppression. Music that began in bondage expanded its expression in a new world. Black art, like Black theology, slowly reset Black identity in America and began to build a legacy.

Which, soon enough, will bring us to hip-hop.

But first, you may be asking what any of this has to do with the old, true story of God's image and our creative call. My answer? Everything. Because in the pressure, injustice, and profound beauty of this journey from the plantation, we see the incredible promise of people who are reclaiming their God-given calling (against all odds) and slowly reimagining life in a broken world.

You see, those old spirituals were more than a distraction to pass the time. Those songs were saturated with coded language to encourage, to instruct, and even to guide toward freedom. Spirituals like "Wade in the Water" and "Swing Low" were instructive anthems for slaves seeking freedom in the North.

These simple songs—just as one example—simultaneously transmitted messages across plantations, expressed praise to God, preserved tradition and folklore, and maintained hope, joy, and perseverance in the face of despair. And in doing this, spirituals—like the rest of true and honest art—reimagined the world that had been forced on the singers. In his book *The Spirituals and the Blues,* James Cone discussed the connection between justice and faith in spirituals: "The slave songs reveal the social consciousness of blacks who refused to accept white limitations placed on their lives."[12]

From the plantation spirituals to Kendrick Lamar's Pulitzer Prize–winning hip-hop, Black art has consistently been a vehicle to transmit these values. On the plantation there were no newspapers or mailmen. Therefore, singing became the go-to way to share news with fellow slaves. And as it grew, hip-hop became a way for people from different neighborhoods or coasts to learn about one another.

When DJ Quik wrote "Jus Lyke Compton" (1992), he was revealing his findings about previously unknown hoods across the country. This was significant for people who wanted to know what Black life was like in communities that were different from theirs. When pioneering West Coast hip-hop group N.W.A brought gangsta rap to the fore of the world's attention with their album *Straight Outta Compton,* the West Coast suddenly became more than its image of sunny beaches and Hollywood allure—another, more honest story was being told, a hard story of police brutality and gang violence.

Aggression in Black creativity was not a new concept that grew out of some inner-city youth revolution. It had been very present on the plantation, where spirituals like "Didn't My Lord Deliver Daniel?" gave vent to the frustration and resistance in the hearts of the oppressed. This gold found in the midst of slavery's shadow gave dimension and depth to Black art. It was real. Slaves were not the passive, dutiful characters some make them out to be. They had a bit of subterfuge in them.

While in recent years gangsta rap's aggressive truth telling often went wrong—turning its aim at its neighbors (rather than the policies that held them under), losing the larger story in an identity of pessimism, or glorifying vice or violence—the shadow of these elements was there because of something valuable. The ability to push back. To tell the truth. To imagine that this world could be better than it is.

Through all this, rappers, like slave singers from generations before, were (and are) wrestling with the big human questions of liberty, land, leadership, and legacy. Who are we to trust if authorities mistreat us? What liberties do I truly have? Do I have space to practice those liberties if Black people are being unfairly policed and killed in our communities? What legacy, outside of poverty and rage, am I to pass down? They were reaching for life beyond their limitations.

The struggle of Black art and expression to find balance among the competing realities of life in an unjust world can direct us all on our creative paths. To harsh realities, harsh truths must be said. In the face of oppression, a holy aggression rises to defend what is good and in danger of being crushed by those who want to dehumanize and exploit. In this way, we come to a crossroads in our creativity. Will we allow God's good creative image to work in us, or will we capitulate to the dishonest, manipulative stories that have echoed since Eden, holding humanity in death and bondage? We must each discern how to respond—whether like Tom or like George, with peaceful acceptance as prophetic witness or with resistance and aggressive truth telling. But that we must respond is certain.

Our gift is meant to be used now, in a world so far from the goodness God intended.

Although freedom gave many people liberty to explore various types of content in their music, songs of adoration and praise were still the most popular in the early twentieth century. As the twentieth century progressed, spirituals and slave songs birthed gospel music. Gospel thrived by combining quartet and jubilee harmonies with blues music for an incredible new sound.

And it thrived because, like the tradition that preceded it, it told the truth. Gospel is a genre as much about longing for justice as about offering praise. Although the majority of the content focused on God, gospel artists often used their platforms to make social or political statements.

Black faith has always been concerned with social issues. From the Free African Society, founded by African Methodist Episcopal preachers Richard Allen and Absalom Jones to provide aid to Africans in need, to Mahalia Jackson publicly supporting Franklin Delano Roosevelt's campaign. What happened in church was intended to move out into the community. There was no divide between the spiritual and the social. And the job of God's people was to bring those two together in story and song.

Supported by the compositions of Thomas Dorsey, Mahalia Jackson would take gospel music to a different level, with the gospel genre becoming just as popular as secular music.

Creativity can make new worlds and new realities. It is about so much more than fantasy or fiction. The slaves found this tool very useful as they labored in a world they knew was corrupt and filled with inequity. Their imagination consisted not just of a hope for heaven but of a hope to see a little of heaven's peace and justice on the earth. Each brave stroke of creativity was a revolutionary act that made a more lucid image of how the world was supposed to be.

Toni Morrison scoffed at the idea of Black people allowing their conditions to cripple their appreciation for art: "What I cannot face is living without my art. . . . I come from a group of people who have always refused to live that way. In the fields we would not live without it. In chains we would not live without it—and we lived historically in the country without *everything,* but not without our music, not without our art."[13]

What makes art essential in this way? Like we've seen—its ability to push against limitations, to describe and critique them. And that's part of why I do what I do as an artist and performer. Just like spirituals, hip-hop is communicating its refusal of limitations.

No rapper has done that better in recent times than

Kendrick Lamar. Lamar's music addresses the human impact of spiritual tensions, much like the apostle Paul did in Romans 7. Each of his albums can be considered a modern-day exposition of the parable of the sower. The spirit is often willing in Lamar, but the flesh is weak. He is contending with the thorns and the Evil One, who desire to choke out the seeds sown in his heart. These are songs written without an evangelical edit; therefore, their language is blunt and appropriate for the culture. We find a perfect example in the song "Alright" (2015), where, in a flow laced with profanity, Lamar sincerely exclaimed,

> *Nazareth, I'm fucked up*
> *Homie, you fucked up*
> *But if God got us, then we gon' be alright*

Why Nazareth? Lamar saw parallels with his homeland, since Nazareth was seen as the "hood" of Jesus's day. Like Lamar's home, Nazareth was associated with poverty. *Surely the Messiah can never come from a poor, despised people such as we are—from Nazareth or any other Galilean town or village!* However, Lamar restored the dignity that was robbed from the territory by preaching God's love for the lowly and marginalized.

Although Lamar started off with a passive Wheatley/Tom theology, he progressed to a more aggressive Walker/George theology:

> *I'm at the preacher's door*
> *My knees getting weak, and my gun might blow*
> *But we gon' be alright*

What's most potent in Lamar's music is his awareness of the plank in his own eye as he points out the plank in others'. There is a way that seems right to Lamar, but he is attempting to flee temptation. He seems to have genuine convictions that lead him to seek theological counsel. He acknowledges his frailty as he seeks understanding of how to handle the injustices of police brutality.

The refrain "we gon' be alright" is both an encouragement to the victim and a proclamation to the victimizer. With the same ethos with which Charles Tindley sang "I'll Overcome Someday," Lamar rapped "Alright." Each became a protest anthem for a generation. Black Lives Matter activists could be seen marching for equality, chanting Lamar's lyrics, just as civil rights leaders sang "We Shall Overcome" in unison.

African American art through history has consistently redeemed and repurposed suffering to promote liberation and hope. Where there was pain, the artist found a means of honest healing. Where there was bondage, the slave found freedom in art.

As much as I felt the angst of my church in 2014, I now better understand the foundation of the disconnect we felt. We had not embraced the same story. The stories we live inform how we see the world. Many Black people see it through plantation eyes. For many Black people, justice is not just a tangential pursuit. Justice is the purpose for which the art is made.

Slavery was a demonic institution. It corrupted the minds of those who endured it and perverted the minds of those who benefited from it and its legacy. When humans fall prey to a dishonest story, there are no winners, not even those "enriched" through manipulation or exploitation.

Despite the brutality of this inhumane system that was meant to purge dignity and suppress creativity, life and creativity blossomed. Only by the grace of God could hope like that endure! This unshaking faith gave Black creativity the opportunity to experience liberation way before emancipation.

But freedom's work is not yet done. The margins are filled with people who require our advocacy and imagination. The legacy of abusive power still remains. There is no earthly condition that can silence the hope and resistance that God places within us. The plantation chains could not contain them. Jim Crow could not mock them. Terror will not shut them up. Systems will not suffocate them.

We are oaks planted by the river. Our limbs may be weak, and the winds may blow, but just know—we gon' be alright.

A LECTURE FROM THE MARGINS

He sat down with a woman soft in frame but strong with words. Here he was, a passionate dilettante, ready to solve her problems. Stating his concerns for the at-risk and marginalized.

Her stare sliced through his ramblings, removing the cancerous confidence with surgical precision.

Although the cut came with pain, it carried enough compassion to correct his naivete. Like most sages, she gave answers through questions. She asked, "Who is marginalized, and who is at risk?" He felt a little disturbed and dismissed, but before he could answer in ignorance, she offered salvation by saying, "I don't have riches, though that would be good. But I have abundance a bank can't cash and dignity no debt can bankrupt.

"My name doesn't grace buildings, though that would be good. But I'm indebted to the many people who have built in me the value of community.

"I don't have a fortune to leave behind, though that would be good. But I will leave a legacy of service and excellence for those who follow."

Then she pivoted by asking, "You may happen to have a fortune and comfort, but is it any good? Do your fortune and power make you more charitable and loving? Next to your stack of resources, is there a stack of opportunities for others? Or do you lock away your resources and keep the combination secure from God?"

She said, "Son, I don't have a combination, a safe, let alone anything to keep protected. All I have, I toss up to heaven, and what falls down is for his children. Be wise, young man, because where thy treasure is, so is thy heart. And thieves are not restricted to the margins."

As her final rebuke, she said, "So, again I ask, Who is at the margins, and who is at risk?"

Maybe we all are. Or maybe a better question is, Who is centered and safe?

4

GUD FOLKS DIS'GREE TOO

Gods always behave like the people who make them.

—ZORA NEALE HURSTON, *Tell My Horse*

For the longest time, I truly believed that family meals—picture perfect, like you saw on TV—were a spiritual discipline. I had heard so many well-meaning saints talk about the value of having a present and attentive family sitting together every night around the dinner table. It felt like a not-so-subtle rebuke to those who didn't practice this.

Now, family dinners are great. But they are also sometimes impractical. We can't assume every house has the time or capacity to have regularly scheduled meals and debriefings. Some parents work nights. Some are too exhausted to have nightly Thanksgiving-worthy meals fully prepped. The absence of family dinnertime, good as it is, does not mean that the family is dysfunctional.

I spent many years living with my grandparents. My grandfather was made out of denim, pragmatism, and few words. His athletic frame intimidated doorways. His hospitality was displayed in his open-door policy for all family members in need. He required only a few personal moments. One of those moments was eating in the solitude of his own thoughts. His tribe of grandkids dared not cross the dining area when he was eating. He rarely ate in the company of others. It could be argued that he was churlish or socially bankrupt, but I would make a different argument. He was a breed of man who greeted the sunrise as he headed to work each day. Dinner was his retreat. He needed a quiet dinner table to maintain his sanity and to love his wife and grandkids, and a quiet dinner table he got.

It's a good idea to eat meals with your family. But that is not the only way to do things. We must not let our good ideas supplant truth. Methods should be a garnish for transcendent truth. What happens when we confuse methods with truth? I'm afraid that much of what is passed off as biblical orthodoxy in some of our spiritual disciplines are simply lifestyle inclinations.

We have to ask as Christians whether the changes we seek to share with the world are those of our culture or of Christ. We must not only work to change the toxic practices of others. We must begin with the inconsistencies in our own practices.

Zora Neale Hurston was an anthropologist and novelist who surveyed many cultures' languages, beliefs, and lifestyles. I'm sure she also observed that, along with creating gods, devotees build temples in honor of those gods—temples that often represent social pressure. People want others to believe like them. They travel around the world on pilgrimages. Some proselytize, sending missionaries to persuade the lost. With full suitcases and good intentions, they enter foreign lands.

I have no intrinsic hate for the work of missionaries. Quite the opposite. I have been blessed by the work of missionaries. I believe that the world should be filled with good ideas and that those ideas should be carried across the globe. But I do believe that missionary work can be misguided.

History shows that missionary projects can become Western colonization disguised as religious compassion. Too often missions has been about the gospel of culture, not the good news of Christ. This points us to an important truth: *if we end up making our God, he'll end up looking like us.*

Now, of course we don't make God. But our perceptions and images of him? That's different. I've seen God painted by believers around the globe: in the bush of Papua, in the quaint towns of Spain off El Camino, in the rural acres of Tuskegee, Alabama, and in the posh cathedrals of London. Each of those locations had a unique but beautiful expression.

But with any image, it's easy to lose the main idea in the details.

Good ideas come in all shapes and sizes. Some of them can transcend cultures.

But what happens when a good idea—a truth even—

becomes a system? Or worse, a *product* advertised to bring you moral or religious absolution? It originates with a particular group—priests, say, or the ruling class or the wealthy—then it slowly reproduces itself. Sometimes this idea removes or renovates even the strongest stories held by a culture. This can be either helpful or dangerous. It all depends on the idea, right? And who's using it and for what.

We've witnessed this principle throughout history. We are still witnessing it now.

So I'll ask a question that may be uncomfortable: *Has this happened to your story?* Could it be that cultural influences—especially influences that benefit some people at the expense of others—have contaminated the good truths that have shaped you? That have shaped your faith?

In my own life, I have seen how deeply Christianity—especially the evangelical exceptionalism that characterizes so much of American Christianity—has been affected by these false stories. Sometimes it feels like we've been in danger of losing the whole point. Losing the very identity that makes us Christian in the first place.

A name can stay even after an identity has been lost. This is one of the great tragedies—and lessons—of gentrification. It's a word that has become extremely popular recently, along with *problematic, woke,* and *influencer.* But in case you're not familiar with it, *Merriam-Webster* defines *gentrification* this way:

> a process in which a poor area (as of a city) experiences an influx of middle-class or wealthy people who renovate and rebuild homes and businesses

and which often results in an increase in property values and the displacement of earlier, usually poorer residents.[1]

Now, stay with me. I'm not addressing a housing crisis here. I believe this concept of gentrification also touches on the displacement of ideas, methods, and practices in many Christian spaces. People who just want to "fix things" can move in and destroy a whole local culture by "helping" it. And this is why Jesus was the greatest neighbor the world has ever witnessed. He invaded our human space without demolishing our culture. Instead, he *raised* the human value of those who were already here. Jesus could break up a party if it defiled his Father's house, but he also brought some "drank" to the wedding, contributing to the celebration. He wasn't here to gentrify. He was here to give us abundant life.

We've already seen how Black art is tethered to justice and how that should influence each of us to create from a space of honesty. Now let's take that further. Because Black artists have not always agreed on what justice ultimately is. Ever since the first slave ship left the coast of West Africa, Black people have had varying ideas on what to do about the Negroes' place in America. Sometimes that variance can get rather uncharitable. This has plagued every Black movement throughout history. Malcolm X berated Martin Luther King Jr. as "a religious Uncle Tom" and said that King's philosophy "plays into the hands of the White oppressors."[2] Claude McKay called Marcus Garvey "a West Indian charlatan."[3] Adam Clayton Powell threatened to fabricate a relationship between King and

Bayard Rustin if they didn't call off a protest at the Democratic National Convention.[4]

I did not grow up in the church. My family did occasionally attend church—when it was convenient—but our regular "worship" happened more in stadiums as we watched my father play football for the New Orleans Saints. Once his playing days ended in the mideighties, our worship transitioned from the stadium to the couch. The same faith, as it were, but different preachers.

As I grew up, one of my older brothers, Dhati, and my father became extremely passionate about their faith. This changed the faith dynamic in our family. Two men I admired loved Jesus and the things that orbited around him. I was forced to go to church and partake in youth group activities. Let me be clear—I loathed it. Unless there was a cute girl to flirt with or a group of people to joke with during services. Some of my greatest obstacles to connecting with what was happening in church were the traditions, practices, and theatrics that seemed peculiar to me.

I was a young man who felt I had progressed beyond what I saw as antiquated theatrics. Thanks to the influence of my oldest brother, Reggie, I was into hip-hop, art house cinema, and Harlem Renaissance poetry. It was not just the traditional Black church I found to be impractical but Christianity in general. What was it *for*? It was a strange world.

Some years later, that faith that I once mocked became my chief affection. The more I matured as a student of history, the more I began to see how the people I loved were influenced by the very faith I mocked. How could I honor and respect those people and their work but ridicule the very thing that inspired them?

When, as a newly converted Christian, I began to go to church on my own terms, I followed my instincts and ushered myself to a traditional Black church—a shouting, whooping, Spirit-filled fellowship. If the "Missionary Baptist" church title didn't indicate that I was entering a *sanctified* church, then the church's location in the deep woods of Opelika, Alabama, should have warned me.

I enjoyed every bit of my year and a half there. But I soon grew discontented. While I was attending this Black church, I was also involved in a weekly small group, which led me to a White church in Montgomery. My newly converted, impressionable Christian mind soon learned of Calvinism and many other Reformed Protestant doctrines. They felt deep and inspiring. I became consumed with the Reformed evangelical world.

What happened next also happened to many of my friends. Maybe even you. Without ever being told this, I gradually began to see one tribe (a subculture of White evangelicalism) as the sole proprietor of Christian growth. After all, why had I not been given this kind of rich theology and heady teaching in the Black church? And it wasn't just doctrines and dogmas that began to form in me— I began to adjust my cultural habits too. Whatever their theologians spoke, I took as authoritative. Whatever cultural practices were significant to them became significant to me. I was completely baptized in what I now see as evangelical exceptionalism—a different, smaller thing than the gospel of Jesus.

Let me be clear: I learned *many* things in those spaces that still benefit me today. However, the most profound principle I learned was not one taught from the pulpit— that a key given by God can be used, even unintentionally, as a chain by people.

I lost my rootedness. My creative life was unbalanced. That is not to say that White Christians cannot be rooted. I've met and still fellowship with many White people who are deeply centered in their theology and lives. But I lost a piece of myself by disdaining my heritage. The history of the Black creative life that had so spoken to me before lost its importance. I disconnected my head from my body. I was still a young Christian, and like all of us, I needed to embrace the fullness of my faith. Both the corporeal and the cognitive gospel.

I became prone to extremes. I lost a little nuance. I projected the shortcomings of that particular church in the woods onto all Black churches. My understanding of Black church history and thinkers was limited. I had no answers to theological challenges or accusations of that tradition. Nor did I have anyone to direct me to different informa- tion. Therefore, Black was simple and baseless. But my understanding would soon change. I found that many of the White pastors and theologians had no "on earth" answers to the plight of those on the margins. When Oscar Grant and Rekia Boyd were unjustly shot by police offi- cers, I received no empathy. When criminal convictions were disproportionately levied on my family and friends, I heard only rebukes. I figured there had to be a gospel that extended empathy along with opposing inequity.

Now, it's just as easy to make improper assumptions about White churches—or the communities of any other cultural tribe. Later, I would discover Protestant, Orthodox, and Catholic churches that all connected their hearts to their heads in the beautiful fullness of the gospel.

Many people are genuinely attempting to improve the lives of others with the practices that bless their own. This can be both gold and shadow. It's similar to gentrification, how the influx of new residents brings new businesses to a neighborhood that formerly was blighted. These new businesses—yoga studios, third-wave coffee shops, upscale grocery stores—are beneficial to the newcomers. They would seem to raise the value of the community. The old residents should appreciate the improvements, right? But have the newcomers thought that what is great for them may not be best for the culture they're invading?

Three major patterns in gentrification can affect creative life as well: economic and social disparities, aesthetic change, and displacement. A neighborhood becomes unbalanced with the first signs of change. Then things begin to really look different. Then the previous inhabitants of the neighborhood are forced out because of the changing economics or culture of the community. It's not that different from what happened to me—seeing the differences between two of the Christian stories I'd been given (and preferring one), then having real changes take place within myself as I accommodated to that new culture. Fortunately, the process was interrupted before a key part of my rootedness and faith had left me entirely.

One way that economic and social disparities are ignored in Christianity is our normalizing of methods from churches with an abundance of resources. We take these methods and attempt to fit them into churches with substantially fewer resources. We assume that every member of that church community has the ability to participate. It can be as simple as attending small groups. I remember a member of my church debating whether he should use his last gallons of gas to attend our weekly small group or use them to get to work the next morning. These types of concerns rocked my Christian paradigm, especially after spending time in a college ministry bubble where being broke was often joked about or romanticized as spiritual.

When Christianity becomes a religion for the privileged, we can begin to selectively accept those biblical principles that best fit our social status. Similar to redistricting a city, we change the rules to the advantage of the powerful. We essentially redefine what is righteous and what is sinful. If these practices continue, then the church will become a homogenous social club. We must be vigilant in resisting a Jesus who seems to say only what we want to hear or a gospel that perpetuates ideals that benefit only our existing cultural structures. No matter who we are, the gospel should challenge us.

When our faith gets gentrified, it also creates aesthetic change—the erosion of the culture that is indigenous to a particular community. As Christians, we should never allow our taste to become too sophisticated for or disconnected from the poor or marginalized. The same people who scorn street art like graffiti must realize that Christian art started with secret vandals in catacombs.

Part of what helps us avoid this internal gentrification is—guess what? An expanded vision of our story. How well do we know our own heritage as Christians? Are we connected to the generations that have gone before us? For example, when we study Christian history in our churches, seminaries, or colleges, how often do we learn of the contributions of Africa and Asia?

In all my Christian academic formation, I never heard the names Gebre Lalibela or King Ezana. I never heard of the Egyptian and Asian Nasara (or Nasraye). I was never informed of the Coptic Christians or Nestorians. The Africanness of Athanasius, Tertullian, Augustine, and others was hardly emphasized. The contributions of believers from across the entire globe were largely omitted in favor of Western teaching. I received the distinct impression that all good Christian systems of thinking came from Europe. If there was a mention of any non-European contribution, it was typically either referred to as deficient or appropriated by a Western counterpart.

Of course, I'm not alone in my experience. When speaking of African contributors to the Christian legacy, Thomas Oden stated, "There is a prejudice at work here: suspect anything of intellectual value that comes from the African continent as having some sort of secret European origin."[5]

Even when we speak of America's contribution to the Christian faith, how often do we hear the names Jarena

Lee, Richard DeBaptiste, Richard Allen, and Anna Julia Cooper referenced in sermons or lectures? Black and White theologians alike can benefit from learning more about these powerful voices of faith. When Black Christians in history are mentioned, they are often seen solely as activists and freedom fighters. These labels are fitting. However, their tendency to use theology to face injustice doesn't diminish their claim to be theologians; it only enhances it. They deserve more than a niche in the library.

I've had the privilege of spending time with Dr. Vince Bantu, who wrote the book *A Multitude of All Peoples*. Dr. Bantu is one of the leading authorities on early Eastern Christianity. In many of our conversations, he has made one thing abundantly clear—that we cannot divorce Christianity from its transformational history that took place in Africa and Asia. The precious time that I have spent with him has freed me from the haunting painting of Norwegian Jesus that hangs in so many homes. Jesus's skin color is not an ultimate truth, but it deeply matters that we can see ourselves in him and see him in ourselves. No portrayal will be perfect, but when we propagate dishonest images of him or his disciples to the exclusion of honest images, we create a psychological weapon. It is much harder to conserve racist and prejudiced ideas when Jesus looks (accurately) more like the people that are being oppressed than their historical oppressors.

Displacement is created through power and means. This is a problem in our churches. We give our platforms to those who are the most successful in the eyes of the world. Conferences and lectures are dominated by individuals who are far removed from the felt needs of many in our communities.

Christianity cannot work for the palace and not the peasant. We need not only a theology of the poor but also a theology *by* the poor. The exalted stories of God's goodness cannot come just from the posh halls of respectable seminaries, but they must also come from the shantytowns of Soweto.

The people who perpetuate these habits can make reconciliation extremely difficult. But the least we can do is create space for understanding and empathy. Christians don't have the luxury of disregarding reconciliation. We cannot ignore truth, pain, or history in favor of a pseudounity. Without truth, there will never be true reconciliation.

If we are going to raise the value of human life without gentrifying the lives of the marginalized, we must appreciate diversity and not appropriate it. The book of Acts is a demonstration of living in the tension of this kind of diversity. The early Christian community struggled with the complexities of ethnicity, persecution history, class, reputation, and geography. But the Spirit gave the church the ability to *excel* in navigating those differences. Their cultural diversity became key to their unity. It was a shining example to the world that there is a God who can bring folks from different experiences together.

That maybe there was a bigger narrative than what they had been told.

When we're starved of accurate Christian history, faces like mine are erased from the pages of our books. We begin to feel that our community's contributions are worthless and that our history is unsophisticated. None of this is true.

When we discover the powerful and diverse faith expressions of the past, we all benefit. I strongly encourage us to do so, working toward a community like the first Christians were able to create. And how do we build toward this? You know what I'm going to say. By creating. By living into a more honest story and then making and working from that place.

When we investigate our past, we learn things of great importance. We become better students and advocates. Toni Morrison stated, "There is infinitely more past than there is future . . . in terms of data."[6] We use our history to make sense of our humanity. This was the role of the old griots, the holy storytellers of West Africa. Their work was to transmit folklore, to keep memory alive.

Zora Neale Hurston stepped into the role of a modern griot with sterling research and deep dignity. Her effort to capture and express the folk culture of the early 1900s American South fueled both anthropological work and a rich body of fiction. Hurston shows us the power of folklore to teach us about God and our world. Folklore is, of course, the "low" culture of a community. It's the art that isn't in museums. The rhymes kids chant that will never grace a bound book. And it can shape us.

Hurston was a master author and a treasure hunter of Negro folklore. She challenged the boundaries of literature in her time. She gave justice to female voices in a way that was unprecedented. She collected countless tales from all over the American South, Haiti, Jamaica, and elsewhere. She brought dignity to people and practices that are often ignored through her collections of folklore and writings such as *Mules and Men, Every Tongue Got to Confess, Dust Tracks on a Road,* and her most popular work, *Their Eyes Were Watching God.*

Hurston was a pillar in the Harlem Renaissance. Centered in the rich 1920s Black culture of New York City's Harlem neighborhood (but extending to multiple northern cities and even to Black communities in Paris), the Harlem Renaissance was a rebirth of African American art. It was a movement of exceptional talent dedicated to expressing a vibrant culture and attacking the racial propaganda of America through creativity. James Weldon Johnson called Harlem "the intellectual and artistic capital of the Negro world."[7]

The Harlem Renaissance gave rise and platforms to icons like Duke Ellington, Louis Armstrong, Josephine Baker, Claude McKay, Alain Locke, Jean Toomer, Ethel Waters, and, of course, Langston Hughes.

Many of the movement's contributors fought racial stereotypes by displaying Black excellence in education, art, and athletics. Hurston's contemporaries worked to exalt the exceptional (often middle-class, educated Negroes) to change wider public opinion. However, Hurston committed her work to a different corner of Black society. She was enthralled by what was perceived as "low" culture, seeking inspiration and information from the ignored and dismissed.

Today in America you will hear discussions about privilege happening everywhere from homes to boardrooms. While racial privilege is a real power dynamic to be discussed, we must not ignore academic and class privilege in the Black community. While still presenting themselves as conduits, those who gain more education and access seem to grow distant from the less educated individuals in the communities they come from. This creates a dangerous dynamic. Often you'll find a small majority of educated activists and pundits making grand claims on behalf of a community that they have no desire to support (reside among or patronize). With the rise of the Black Lives Matter movement, you would think by the noise made on social media and news networks that there is overwhelming support among Black Americans for defunding or abolishing the police. However, recent research done by Gallup has shown that 61 percent say otherwise.[8] This is why it's imperative to give voice to the margins.

A dominant culture tends to dismiss what it perceives as undereducated. Take oral tradition for example. It's easy enough to look down on tales passed from person to person as ignorant or superstitious, right? But in cultures founded on oral tradition, there is an expectation of rigorous accuracy and trustworthiness. And just to point out a double standard, have we not made the ancient folklore of

Christianity academic? To many of their original hearers, the tales of a virgin-born Messiah who died on a cross only to resurrect three days later sounded like the ravings of lunatics. The stories dissected in seminaries around the world today have their deepest roots in holy (and trustworthy) folklore.

And it's this oral tradition that Hurston's work honored and preserved. I don't want to romanticize Hurston's theology. Her personal beliefs were complicated. But she was a genius in her hermeneutic of people.

She captured ordinary people who believed in a personal God but sat outside the circles of power. Ordinary people like the family matriarch, Nanny, in *Their Eyes Were Watching God,* who says, "Ah wanted to preach a great sermon about colored women sittin' on high, but they wasn't no pulpit for me."[9] Nanny goes on to profess that she found her pulpit in the rearing of the story's protagonist, Janie. She is a heroine who raises a heroine.

As Janie gets older, we see her gathering the courage to challenge the misogyny around her. After being the target of many jokes, Janie becomes empowered and challenges the degrading banter. One line that I find particularly strong is a theological statement she makes among jesting men:

Sometimes God gits familiar wid us womenfolks
too and talks His inside business.[10]

Hurston was using Janie to push against a world of patriarchy and sexism. She brings God, the ultimate authority on the subject of being, into the conversation.

Janie is suggesting that God uses women for his business as well as those more centered in power. And the Bible affirms this. Esther saved lives with her selfless acts. The interaction between Jesus and the woman at the well led to great revival. Mary Magdalene and two other women became the first proclaimers of the good news. Janie is basically saying, "I may be on the margins of society, but God knows where to reach me."

Hurston was revolutionary in liberating Janie on the page and thus liberating Black female readers across the country. However, she did much more than liberate female readers. She redirected attention to the overlooked stories on the margins and how powerfully they are used by God.

Hurston removed the veil from high society so they could see the rest of the world as God sees it. Much of her work demonstrates the tension between high society and low culture, academia and oral traditions.

The creative life isn't just relegated to our artistic expressions. Our lives are in themselves creative. And so are the lives of others, if we can learn to listen to them.

But too often background, class, and status distract us from receiving the essence of what someone is saying. We become distracted from the truth because of our prejudice about whom or where it's coming from. But as linguist John McWhorter explained, form doesn't necessarily disrupt meaning.[11]

Hip-hop is often perceived as low art in comparison

with the work of Shakespeare or Euripides, even when it employs similar literary devices like polyptota, rhetorical questions, double entendres, alliteration, similes, and more. One is "literature," and one is not. Why?

In many ways, the highbrow church and the "sanctified" church that I attended in my younger days were espousing the same truths. Though I was attracted to theological acumen, I hadn't been able to fully appreciate the theology that was present in the church I had left. The two congregations, in the big picture, were painting much the same picture. But they were using different colors. If you ain't on dis, then let me remind ya. Listen to a few of these "low" expressions of the profound theological truths that I later came to appreciate so deeply.

"Hold on to God's unchanging hands." In the halls of a prestigious seminary, that would be identified as expressing the immutability of God. Whether in the fields of Mississippi or in the classrooms of Princeton, this doctrine explains that God's promises and perfection are unchanging.

"The blood done signed my name." In a highbrow church, this would be called "substitutionary atonement." This saying is explaining the way the sacrificial Lamb gave me his righteousness, setting me right with God.

"Keep on keepin' on!" Some of you would call this "the perseverance of the saints." This exhortation is encouraging the saints to work out their salvation with fear and trembling.

Or, to bring this full circle, we can listen to the character Charlie Jones's reverence in *Their Eyes Were Watching God*: "Lawd, Lawd, Lawd . . . it must be uh recess in heben if St. Peter is lettin' his angels out lak dis!"[12] Charlie is preaching a sermonette on the *imago Dei,* affirming the beauty of God's creation.

And I am so glad I can hear him now.

The world is broken. We who are made in the image of the Creator are working to change that. But sometimes the challenges are daunting. How can we find our voices without losing ourselves? How can we work to change the world without making it in our image (gentrifying it)—turning others into hollow versions of ourselves? How can we release our gifts with power and inspire others to go and do likewise?

True creativity isn't about sameness. We approach problems in various ways as members of the human family. Some preach change in big words from podiums set before dignitaries. Others sit with the uneducated in scorching southern fields. Jesus is with both. I serve the Christ of both.

We are each a written letter that's still being edited. We are concerned about being misinterpreted. There is a popular saying in my community: "Black people are not a monolith!" and we celebrate that diversity . . . until it knocks up against our DJ table and disrupts our rhythm. When a truth becomes inconvenient, what you do next is what reveals your character. Many of us would rather chastise the disrupters of our stereotypes than allow for true diversity. But that is not the change we need.

This is not just a Black problem. The various "social clubs" we belong to can create tacit expectations that marginalize people. It's the nature of tribes. In addition to that, within tribes there are tribes. And it is virtually impossible for people to have the same opinion on every meaningful issue. Furthermore, when someone holds to an ideology that is different from ours, we want to assume the worst of that person. Anna Julia Cooper touched on how we can appropriately deal with difference: "A nation or an individual may be at peace because all opponents have been killed or crushed; or, nation as well as individual may have found the secret of true harmony in the determination to live and let live."[13]

As my friend John Onwuchekwa often says, "A cease-fire is good because it brings peace, but God desires for enemies to be family." I hope to lay my gun down and reason with the sensible arguments of my brother rather than worrying about dodging bullets. I have meaningful relationships with people who hold "memberships" with various social clubs. They all say they want the same outcome, but there is a diversity of opinions on how to achieve it. Garvey, Hurston, Cooper, Du Bois, McKay, and others all professed similar desires to see justice for Black people, but they sharply differed on the means. They agreed on the what but never reached a consensus on the how.

We are human beings driven by self-interest. We desire communities but not at the sacrifice of our own interest and desires.

Is this not the problem of America? Are we not all in need of grace? I know I am a person who has a toxic past and I am clumsy in the present. The majority of us are neither heroes nor villains. We are bystanders trying to interpret the times.

We all have our own ideas of what exceptional behavior looks like. We also tend to measure the world by those metrics. However, are those metrics in line with the gospel? Are we expecting a man who has worked from dawn to dusk to have the energy to engage a pack of kids in the twilight hours of the day? Do we think that people with little education have less understanding than the gentry? Do we expect David to be comfortable in Saul's armor? Some of our expectations can create progressive change. But others paint God in our image.

Toward the conclusion of *Their Eyes Were Watching God,* Janie is facing trial for killing her husband in self-defense. As she stands before her accusers and advocates, the narrator details what she is struggling with the most: "It was not death she feared. It was misunderstanding."[14]

We all desire to be understood. We want to be seen. The way to affirm dignity isn't solely to prop up exceptional people. Anyone can love exceptional people. The gospel is real when we find ourselves loving our neighbors who don't fit our careful constructs. Our goal shouldn't be uniformity. It should be dignified tension and learning. On both sides.

This is Jesus crossing through Samaria. This is Peter eating with Cornelius the centurion.

Gentrification often comes with many benefits like new developments and an increase in community value; however, it can ultimately lead to a loss of identity. The same happens in our creative life when we expect class shift or the prestige of academia to increase our worth. Higher education and income don't equate to a greater comprehension of what is good. When I've sought the approval of people, I've often discovered that I become a terrible version of them that may never be fully integrated into this foreign society.

Furthermore, the most important quality to maintain is spiritual centeredness. I was enamored with the praise and rewards given to me by those who wanted me to be their cultural critic. My feet almost slipped because I lacked the centeredness of many of my biblical heroes. Without a proper centeredness, internal gentrification would have consumed Moses, Daniel, and Esther. They recognized the luxury at their disposal in the palace, but they never let the luxury define them or their calling. I still frequent the palaces of Christianity and academia. I've tasted their wines, and I've learned their cultures. I know how to operate around kings and queens. I can seek the flourishing of Babylon as Jeremiah instructed without turning away from my God.[15] Gentrification may come, but I will never lose the prophetic voice in my heart. Besides, I do not like the god they have made.

5

THE GOOD EXILES

When we come to Christ . . . , Jesus does not ask
us to abandon our sin-stained culture in order to
embrace someone else's sin-stained culture.

—RICHARD TWISS, *One Church, Many Tribes*

I was placed in a papyrus basket and sent down the I-20 river. I was drawn out of the basket by the welcoming arms of evangelicalism. I found life in the palace pleasing and comforting. However, I began to learn of my origins. I am of Eden. We all are of Eden. A place full of joy, solidarity, and flourishing.

Our people left Eden many years ago. Our greed and lust for autonomy led us away from being satisfied with perfection. Now we wander. There are tales of a return. Those tales often seem as implausible as the fact that Eden ever existed. Our present residences are erasing the memory of a better home. We are like orphans hoping the stars will help us navigate back but not knowing how to read them.

Since God's people have been expelled from Eden, many of the dispersed have attempted to recreate it. Some fully embrace their position as ambassadors in a foreign land. Some still wander, knowing they will never find contentment on this side of heaven. Some know this earth is passing away but have built kingdoms that carry a lot of authority.

Many Black Christians who would call themselves evangelicals are spiritual orphans attempting to make a life in a foreign land. Defining exactly what makes someone an evangelical has proven to be a difficult task, especially in the present climate. *Evangelical* is a word that carries many competing definitions today, particularly when used in a political context. These four components of evangelicalism by David Bebbington represent my understanding of what constitutes evangelical belief:

Conversionism: the belief that lives need to be transformed through a "born-again" experience and a lifelong process of following Jesus

Activism: the expression and demonstration of the gospel in missionary and social reform efforts

Biblicism: a high regard for and obedience to the Bible as the ultimate authority

Crucicentrism: a stress on the sacrifice of Jesus Christ on the cross as making possible the redemption of humanity[1]

Bebbington's categories sound like many traditional Black churches. However, most of them would not consider themselves evangelical. Generally, Black Christians are *labeled* evangelical by others because of their proximity to and dependence on White Christians and institutions.

Many Black evangelicals see themselves as modern-day recipients of Jeremiah's prophetic instructions to "seek the welfare of the city" as exiles.[2] That term can use a little explanation these days, but it's one of the most important ideas in the biblical story. *Exile* is what happens in the Bible when God's people are displaced by circumstances beyond their control and find themselves in strange surroundings. *Exile* is having to deal with the consequences of decisions made generations ago. *Exile* is trying to find your footing when you barely know which way is down. *Exile* is having little other than the memory of your oldest story that is keeping your hope for the future alive. *Exile* is a desire for home and the knowledge that you may never see it.

Now, here's the thing: we're all exiles. The Bible is clear that this world is not the Christian's home. And it is also clear that we are to do our best to spruce it up a little bit. No matter your situation, God has intentionally placed you in a particular position to be a blessing. This is where your gifts and work come to bear. You are to live into this calling here. And now.

To quote one of the great biblical prophets writing to Israel during their exile and slavery in a foreign land, we are to "build houses . . . plant gardens and eat their produce. Take wives and have sons and daughters."[3] But don't get too comfortable, of course. This world is still in need of repair.

There is always the threat of being "Daniel'd" in a lion's den when we go against the popular thought of the society that surrounds us. There is nothing easy about living faithfully, and when we commit ourselves to remembering and telling the greatest story honestly, we set ourselves against powerful forces that want to silence us.

Yes, God is our Father. That relationship is secure and potent. But our condition doesn't always feel that way. We're tasked with making our way in a world that is jarring. No matter where we orphans find ourselves, we should attempt to make our society better than it currently is. The orphans of Eden bring paradise with them.

God placed me, an orphan of Eden, on a stage in the Christian music industry. The stage, for many creatives, is like a home. Its hospitality can be intoxicating. When you step on it, you find yourself in the presence of people who are ready for recess in your imaginative playground. The euphoria of performing is unmatched. Waves of affirmation stimulate your dull senses. The stage offers a currency the whole globe holds as legal tender: *attention.*

But the stage can also be a very complicated place. As long as spectators are entertained, they will applaud. Applaud the right. Applaud the wrong.

The stage has presence, but it has no personality. It has only what you bring to it. The stage is a mirror that reflects the confidence and insecurities of the artist who steps on it. It doesn't set the agenda. It's just a meeting place, an address where the artist and the audience have decided to meet and make an exchange. It could be a palace of comfort, or it could be a haunted house. The audience may bring their expectations to this communal gathering like nosy neighbors. These expectations may torment the artist. The artist can choose to embrace these expectations or expel them to keep the stage unencumbered.

At some point in our creative life, we will each have to ask ourselves a set of questions: *What is my Eden? If I am in exile, how can I "seek the welfare of the city" while keeping my dignity?*

The early years of my Christian faith found me in a palace. But in 2010, that stage in the palace began to haunt me. This was one year after my sophomore release, *Lions and Liars,* which was quite a success for an independent label. I received a Stellar Award nomination and landed a Billboard spot. The recognition of my hard work felt encouraging.

But the intoxication quickly turned into an excruciating hangover. The limitations I felt in the Christian music industry suffocated my creativity. It seemed as if someone had commissioned me to paint but the canvas was a finished product. I wanted the applause and affirmation, but I didn't want to lose myself in the process.

My label mates and I were swooned over by prominent pastors and Christian institutions that saw us as rapping recruiters for a culture war that needed urban credibility. No matter how well-intentioned they were, I was no longer willing to be a mercenary. We felt the burden of fitting into the monolithic cultural mold of evangelicalism. Eden was almost forgotten.

I needed freedom to explore. Freedom to celebrate the

icons I once read and to address the issues within the palace. Freedom to speak on the matters pertinent to me that didn't make it through the evangelical edit. I wanted freedom to expose the darkest corners of society at large without facing the concern that these dark deeds would infect me or the consumer.

That meant I had to either be brave enough to speak truth to power or exit the palace altogether. Once again, I began to ask myself a series of questions: *What does it mean to be a Christian artist? Who sets that precedent? Does the present Christian culture promote spiritual redemption or cultural assimilation? Should we even have a "Christian industry," and if so, what are we doing right, and what are we doing wrong?*

Then it all came to a head. I remember a series of events that drove me from making music that was acceptable to the contemporary Christian music (CCM) and gospel markets. I felt CCM and gospel didn't allow artists to be honest about the gold and shadow of society. We couldn't fully celebrate the gold. And we were expected to handle sex, social activities, and any worldly association like Puritan pastors.

The shadow of society was rarely handled maturely. We often discussed immorality in culture only when it benefited our political agenda or social arguments.

I had already been frustrated with responses to the spoken-word piece "I'm Black" on my album *Lions and Liars,* performed by my good friend Adam Thomason. The piece is nothing more than a critique of the social constructs that promote racial divides. It is tame compared with some of my later work. I was also heartbroken by the death of my fellow California native Oscar Grant at the hands of police. I felt like the Christian stages I was occupying were not willing to dialogue about these types of issues. Add the puzzling detail that the majority of the audiences at our tour stops and festivals were White conservative teens and college students who had a very different background than I had. I felt the winds blowing whenever difficult conversations occurred. We were different tribes meeting in the metropolis.

Imagine me before this crowd. I was raised in California by a mother who was an active participant in the Black Panther Party. My parents consistently encouraged me to read literature from Black authors and do projects about Black figures and movements in history. At a very young age, I became enamored with poetry because of their encouragement to read Langston Hughes and other figures from the Harlem Renaissance. I attended Tuskegee University because I wanted to attend a historically Black university.

I began to ask myself, *How did I end up on this stage?* My biggest song from that album was a track celebrating marriage. I would guess that 90 percent of my audience at that time was not married. I was trying to "seek the welfare" of that audience, but honestly, I preferred an exodus. This exodus was not simply for racial or cultural purposes but for creative liberation. I felt a call to be a little less exiled. To see whether there was anything left of my homeland out there.

The Hebrew people and the Exodus have been compared ad nauseum with Black liberation in America.

However, let me use the Exodus in a way that might be slightly novel.

I believe four essentials will aid us in our journey as orphaned Black evangelicals. First, no redemption or liberation will come through passivity. There must be *leadership* called to put themselves in compromising situations for the good of others. People who are willing to call for the rebuilding of the city. Yahweh chose Moses, a man who had an intimate understanding of Egyptian life and practices. However, he was of the people and not the palace.

Second, God *liberates* his people. Liberation is safety from physical and psychological enslavement. God communicated his intentions to Moses in Exodus 3:

> The LORD told him, "I have certainly seen the oppression of my people in Egypt. I have heard their cries of distress because of their harsh slave drivers. Yes, I am aware of their suffering. So I have come down to rescue them from the power of the Egyptians and lead them out of Egypt into their own fertile and spacious land.[4]

Liberation without land, literal or metaphorical, will intensify the tension between the powerful and the marginalized. This is a call to institutions that encourage the voices of Black evangelicals. This point is also pertinent to creatives who exist in spaces that suffocate their voices. There is no utopia, but there are spaces that present fewer obstacles to you feeling dignified. Freedom fighters like Mandela and King knew that land meant money and power. What good is it to be free with limited access to resources?

Third, God establishes a *law*. He doesn't liberate his people to be reckless and lawless. He knew that the laws and practices of Egypt were flawed and idolatrous. God couldn't allow Moses to lead his nation into a new land with the laws of their oppressor. This means that some principles from the palace may not be beneficial for the work we have before us. We may need new faith practices, new business principles, and new relational guidelines.

Last, God gives his people a *legacy*. After the Exodus, God re-formed Israel's identity, which had been damaged during slavery. In Exodus 4, he gave a reason that this oppression was unacceptable:

> You will tell him, "This is what the LORD says: Israel is my firstborn son. I commanded you, 'Let my son go, so he can worship me.'"[5]

Our liberation gives us freedom to create. Freedom to worship God with our lives, work, and relationships. Freedom to be a testament to godly relationships on earth. Freedom to use our unique gifts to make this place a little more like Eden.

Many Black evangelicals like me have to begin to be honest about why we assimilate in White evangelical spaces even when we know we'll feel like orphans. For creatives, assimilation can be financially rewarding, and we may receive social plaudits as authoritative voices in spaces of limited diversity. But it can also feel like an exile within an exile. If we're asking Pharaoh to fund our endeavors, we should also expect to make the kind of art that's fitting for Egypt. Egypt has its own battles to fight. If you accept their stage, then you also accept their battles. I found that I couldn't always make those fights my own.

Black evangelicals have had this problem for decades. I accepted the gold and shadow in this dilemma that had been felt by artists like Christian hip-hop forerunners Stephen Wiley, Michael Peace, Preachers in Disguise, Dynamic Twins, Gospel Gangstaz, and SFC.

Before I ever knew that I was an exile or that I would desire to pursue a career in the Christian music market, I witnessed something quite amazing. My life was forever changed in 1998 when I saw seven emcees address an Atlanta audience like Paul at the Areopagus. My eyes were fixed on something celestial. My mind couldn't quite comprehend what was happening before me. I found griots and poets from a new tribe. I wouldn't be the same man once I ascended from this baptismal experience presented by the urban-ecclesiastical Cross Movement. They connected a culture I loved dearly to my newfound faith. My senses were overwhelmed.

Confidence and conviction shot out of their mouths:

It's only right that we get our Christ on . . .
No blood, no forgiveness
Not a smidgen
Without the blood, kid, you only got religion[6]

The Cross Movement was a melody from heaven to my newly saved ears. They moved as if they'd just departed the Broad Street Line. They spoke with accents and colloquialisms that reminded me of *my* neighborhood. They rhymed with precision and confidence. This was no suburban gimmick attempting to be authentic.

The Cross Movement consisted of the Tonic (John Wells), the Ambassador (William "Duce" Branch), Phanatik (Brady Goodwin), T.R.U.-L.I.F.E (Virgil Byrd), Cruz Cordero, Enock (Juan James), and Earthquake (Cleveland Foat). This motley crew of personalities hailed from all over the East Coast. Many appropriately dubbed them "a Christian Wu-Tang."[7]

See, sometimes you just need an example to set you free. These gentlemen were endearing because they addressed religious tensions in the urban context. Their posture and approach gave many young people like myself cultural affirmation and biblical insight. Before the expansion of Christian hip-hop (CHH), the most relevant Christian artist was Kirk Franklin. As much as I love to "stomp," Franklin was *not* filling the void left by mainstream hip-hop.

Let me be clear—the Cross Movement was not the standard for all Christian hip-hop. It was just the standard for *me*. The members were prophets and poets for orphaned Black evangelicals. Despite their legacy and the projects they launched, however, they have no real equity or influence in the Christian music industry today. Unlike in CCM, Black evangelicals in CHH have little to no control over distribution and have no significant festivals or talent agencies that represent their interest. This is a shame when many of these artists help build the palace, but they have no home!

These gentlemen who embraced the culture of hip-hop and fidelity to the Bible were not self-produced. The blessing of the Cross Movement can be placed in the lineage of a burgeoning movement of Black evangelicals in the sixties. One of those Black evangelicals was Tom Skinner, a former New York gang member and the son of a preacher, who became an urban evangelist and social critic. He was like a Malcolm X for young Black Christians who sought a gospel that spoke to both the corporeal and the cognitive.

Tom Skinner was more than a preacher and social critic. He ran multiple institutions that focused on leadership development. He was the chaplain for the Washington Redskins for many years and was said to have influential relationships with prominent athletes, musicians, and other public figures. But what most distinguished Skinner was his understanding of the gospel. He wrote multiple books about Christianity and its tumultuous place in a post-civil-rights Black America.

The civil rights movement of the fifties and sixties had created a new expectation of integration. Many White and Black Christians used these times as an opportunity for reconciliation. College ministries like InterVarsity and Campus Crusade for Christ (now Cru) were hosting frequent conferences and attracting droves of Black students. Many Black evangelicals were focused on integration into these White institutions. While many orphans were finding homes, Tom Skinner was a sobering voice in the wild. During his infamous message at InterVarsity's Urbana '70, Skinner affirmed Black identity and critiqued White evangelicalism:

It was not the evangelical who came and taught us
our worth and dignity as black men. It was not the
Bible-believing fundamentalist who stood up and
told us that black was beautiful. . . . Rather, it took
Malcolm X, Stokely Carmichael, Rap Brown and
the Brothers to declare to us our dignity.[8]

Unsatisfied with the obligatory breakout sessions and
empty attempts at "speaking to African Americans' core
concerns,"[9] Skinner's team, Bill Pannell, and Carl Ellis Jr.
decided to host their own gatherings on the East Coast.

Following the model set by Tom Skinner Associates,
young Black leaders led a new wave of conferences. Some
were held under the authority of White institutions, while
others were autonomous.

In 1975, Charles "Chuck" Singleton, a director with
the intercultural branch of Campus Crusade, organized
Harambe Holiday in Chicago. The aim was to reach a
greater audience than just college students. Harambe
rolled out a who's who of the Black Christian world, including forty pastors. In attendance were Jesse Jackson, Andraé
Crouch, and E. V. Hill, and Tom Skinner led an outreach
event. Harambe Holiday hosted over eight hundred attend-
ees during the Fourth of July holiday.[10] However, this
would be the only Harambe conference.[11]

This vibrant crop of Black ministers including Haman
Cross Jr., Crawford Loritts, Thomas Fritz, Matthew Parker,
and Elward Ellis organized another gathering of Black
evangelical preachers, ministers, and musicians who aimed
to reach Black college students for the purpose of spiritual
development. This event was called Chicago '81. Once

again, though the event was a success, there would be no second conference.

This newfound interest in parachurch ministries led Charles Gilmer and Thomas Fritz to launch an auxiliary ministry of Campus Crusade called the Impact Movement. The goal of the Impact Movement was to reach Black students with biblical truth by way of a cultural expression that was true to their experience.

It was at an Impact Conference that I became a Christian and witnessed the Cross Movement marry hip-hop authenticity and biblical fidelity. That Atlanta night in 1998 became an identity-forming experience.

Author, professor, and theologian Dr. Carl Ellis Jr. started his journey with Tom Skinner in 1969. Ellis also studied under Francis Schaeffer at L'Abri Fellowship. Ellis believes that many Black evangelicals during that time fell into one of two categories. There were those who were determined to be *assimilationist* and those who were *identificationalist*. Of course, all categories are nuanced with individuals landing on various parts of the spectrum.

The extreme assimilationists were those who desired to adopt ideologies and methods from White institutions. They often even encouraged integration into White institutions, believing this was best for individual and communal progress.

The identificationalists developed ideas and methods that focused on the identity and institutions unique to their culture.

Ellis believes that many of his contemporaries, as well as Skinner, were identificationalists who hoped to bring change within White evangelical spaces. However, at some point identificationalists wear down the institution and end up being orphaned again.

Skinner recognized that the more Black Christians assimilated into White spaces, the less likely they would be to ever discover true independence or hear a message of hope that would affirm Blackness.

> Rather than empowering themselves, African Americans pursued the illusive dream of integration, and it is destroying us. . . . Under segregation we built and were in charge of our own institutions. We ran our own schools, built our own banks, and started our own colleges. Under segregation we did not have to use words like "role models" because that's what everyone was in the African American community. In my neighborhood, Duke Ellington, James Baldwin, Thurgood Marshall, Adam Clayton Powell, Jr., Malcolm X, Jackie Robinson were everyday common occurrences on our streets. When integration came, it meant that those who could afford it and qualified were integrated into white society, while the rest stayed behind. Thus we needed role models. When integration occurred, the black leaders of the black community integrated into the white community. But they were never allowed to hold the same positions of leadership and power that they held in the black community.[12]

As long as Black evangelicals were "preaching the gospel," they received many rewards. Once they ventured to affirm Blackness and build systems, they were quickly labeled radicals.

Tom Skinner would face his own obstacles. In 1973, his college ministry division fell apart after replacing key leaders like Bill Pannell and Carl Ellis Jr.

Also, Skinner's divorce from his first wife, Vivian, left a stain on his reputation with many White evangelical institutions. He became less of a darling and more of a disgrace. It didn't help that his second wife, Barbara Williams-Skinner, was connected to the Congressional Black Caucus, which nauseated the mostly conservative White evangelical ministries. Despite his shortcomings, however, Tom Skinner was the prophetic voice in the wilderness who found himself between Egypt and Eden.

Some Black evangelicals continued as sojourners, while others found their homes. But no matter whether they continued to wander or whether they sought the welfare of White institutions, they remained orphans.

Being a creative orphan is not a novel concept. And every so often, enough orphans get together that a movement is started—a collective creative project that carries profound promise. You can't manufacture it. Remember the Harlem Renaissance? It was arguably the most significant cultural movement of artists, thinkers, and activists to originate on American soil.

The Harlem Renaissance was more than a movement that gave the world social products. It was a fight for racial dignity, economic control, and political solidarity. Behind the art and literature were powerful arbitrators making decisions that would determine the success of this unprecedented movement.

It is proof that no matter how exceptional the Black mind may be, when left without institutional control and resources to execute their aspirations, Black people will consistently be mercenaries for those in power. They were brilliant. But like so many other creatives in exile, they were also used.

In *The Crisis of the Negro Intellectual,* Harold Cruse observed that the talented citizens of Harlem were unable to make substantive changes to the world around them, despite their profound talent and hard work. "What they desperately wanted to be able to do," he wrote, "was to assume absolute control of Harlem affairs in economics, politics and culture, but they could not."[13] The artists and social thinkers of the Harlem Renaissance failed to produce economic, political, and social institutions of power or positive change. They made cultural products but never found a home that would appreciate them. Their art lives on, but did it live up to its potential? Arguably, it did not.

Just as White conservatives control entertainment outlets within Christian music from Los Angeles to Nashville, White Marxists controlled Harlem's entertainment epicenters of the time (the Lafayette and Lincoln Theaters[14]) and the political strategies influencing the community.

Claude McKay, a poet and activist, recognized that Black Americans needed to push for a Black political structure. Cruse critiqued McKay, however, for understanding the need for political solidarity but not taking responsibility to educate the masses through his art.[15]

Not only were the geniuses of Harlem subjected to left-wing political influence without having influence of their own, but they were also financed by eccentric White liberals who found a new hobby in patronizing Negro art, such as Mabel Dodge and Emilie Hapgood.[16] Cruse stated that, "having no cultural philosophy of their own, they remained under the tutelage of irrelevant white radical ideas. Thus they failed to grasp the radical potential of their own movement."[17]

If we investigate the landscape of Black evangelicalism and Christian hip-hop, we will find that these movements, like the Harlem Renaissance, lack a collective philosophy, economic initiative, and political strategy, as well as the institutional weight to execute real change.

What were the causes of cultural disintegration in Harlem? I find that Harlem, Tom Skinner, and Christian hip-hop faced similar obstacles that kept their cultural products from creating leadership, liberty, law, and legacy.

This shows us that we need to be vigilant not only in the beginning of our journey toward God-given creative freedom but also in all the practical steps along the way. If we want to see change and the honest expression of our creative work, we must give the best we have and seek a structure that will allow our best to flourish.

Let me examine my own work as a music artist with this in mind. Christian hip-hop artists, like Black evangelicals, must value their cultural product as unique. Once we see it and ourselves as unique—exiles within an exile—we will begin to realize that we might need our own institutions and spaces in order to thrive. There is much benefit in being an orphan. You are able to transcend cultures well. You have the ability to evaluate homogenous contexts through a heterogeneous lens. But there is also danger—the shadow of being lost in the majority culture or even becoming a token. White patronage is good and welcomed. However, too many Black creatives, thinkers, and movements have collapsed because of their dependency on White patronage.

I have felt this tension. No matter who you are, you might have experienced some aspect of this tension as well. Our job is to allow ourselves to long for a space of honest expression and then be willing to step toward it. There is nothing easy about this. We can renovate a home for only so long before we grow exhausted. We have to rest at some point.

The Harlem Renaissance was a significant movement. But I wonder what more it could have become. Can you imagine if there had been real solidarity and trust between the artists of the movement and those who controlled the means of distributing their art? I believe we would experience a different America today. But both dishonesty and division will make a real movement irrelevant. Eventually, in spite of talent and energy, it will disintegrate.*

Ultimately, what we exiles need is the same honesty that we used to reclaim the beginning of our story in Eden.

---

* Even though Christian hip-hop carries an inconsequential portion of the potential the Harlem Renaissance had, I believe it can still have great impact in the Christian community. Christian hip-hop is a real movement. But we must act swiftly before irrelevance becomes disintegration.

We must look honestly at the promise of the future. In *The Spirituals and the Blues*, James Cone presented four points about Black eschatology that I believe can assist Christian hip-hop and Black evangelicals toward the resolution we seek.[18]

(1) *Historical possibilities.* Can we excel? Is our welfare (economic, political, and social) possible in a foreign land? How was it achieved in the past, and what can we learn from that achievement?

(2) *Limited possibilities.* How do we maintain dignity in the face of limited possibilities? Cone stated that when "slaves realized that their historical possibilities were limited, they began to create structures of black affirmation which protected their humanity even though they could not escape the chains of slavery."[19] Out of this hope came spirituals, folklore, and cakewalking. Today hip-hop uses fashion, dancing, slang, and a variety of other mediums to bring dignity to a marginalized community. If we are to be exiled, how do we create using mediums that bring dignity and that are both culturally relevant and biblical?

(3) *Life after death.* Although we face many problems on earth, we must ultimately find our reward in an eternity with God. However, we don't ignore our present conditions. We must ask ourselves, *Does my eschatology address the comprehensive evils of the world?* The emergence of Christian hip-hop

has created an interesting opportunity for artists to reclaim the ingredients that made the spirituals a unified cognitive and corporeal art. Somehow the subgenre has so far failed in that task.

(4) *Historicity.* Cone suggested that, despite how our history may unfold, Black Christians have an ultimate hope that transcends our present circumstances. God will be our deliverer despite history's track of injustice. As stated in the introduction, the Black evangelical comes from a tradition rooted in resilience and hope. We have been orphans for many years. However, we do not accept an identity of pessimism. We live in the already but not yet.

Be mindful that I do not preach separatism here. But I do encourage an appropriate autonomy for people who make cultural products. Some of our actions require us to be reformist, and some require us to be revolutionary. The gospel is both confrontational and unifying. Let's remember that, whether in the palace or in the desert, we may still be orphans.

I recognize now that, in trying to step away from spaces that constrained my voice, I wasn't leaving Egypt; I was just leaving the palace. I recognize that, at a practical level, there may be no escaping Egypt. If there can be no return to Eden or exodus toward a promised land, we can only try to shine the light of God and change the heart of Pharaoh and hope that when he dies, the succeeding Pharaoh will be good.

I am an artist. I come from a place. I am a storyteller who loves God and loves how his creation has used raw materials to bless the world. I am a storyteller who wants an audience to engage and a home where I can be my complete self. I acknowledge the difficulty of finding that home.

This place, this world, is responsible for shaping my ideas and work. We can't ignore the environments that developed us. We are the personification of our communities. When we move, we bring history and home with us. We are the beautiful buds that benefit from the nourishment of the roots.

We are griots and ambassadors traveling, sharing our stories about a foreign land. Some of our development is marred with transgressions—ours and others'.

Praise be unto God that he is redeeming all the broken areas of our character and place.

Praise be unto God that redemption isn't replaced with assimilation.

Praise be unto God that moral uprightness doesn't mean taking off my culture and putting on another.

I seek a better land, a better city. As I pursue my true home, God has given me the task of seeking the welfare of the city where I now live. While I'm an orphan on earth, I can have no greater satisfaction than knowing that I'm a citizen of heaven. We will soon learn that there is no returning to the Garden of Eden. However, there is a Garden of Gethsemane. A place for rest and supplication in the midst of pain and confusion. As I seek the welfare of this city, I pray God affirms my work *and sees that it is good.*

And I pray the same for you.

THE MOON MAN

If you tune your ears, you might hear the echoes of an old parable. Though the details have been lost or changed through generational exchange, the essence has remained.

There was a young merchant who traveled from the big city. He had heard great tales of Le Ville Noir, the Black City. Being a Black man himself, he felt he must visit this city. He considered his trade and figured that selling to Aunt Hagar's children would be an easy way to get his hands on a few nickels. Who in this city could resist his allure and charisma? His time around White folks had prepared him for such a campaign.

He grabbed his best threads but soon discovered that his fashion wasn't impressive in the least. The whole city dressed as if they were waiting for an invite to some dignitary's gala. He was bemused by their quiet confidence.

The merchant needed to reconstruct his confidence. He figured he had learned from the best. He was a city boy who worked under White men. Let me inform you that *under* is the essential word. He did not know that the Negroes in Black City never had to look up to anyone. Nevertheless, he was not going to be intimidated. He figured they were peacocks but he could fly.

He first approached the general store and his fellow merchants. "The good people of this town could do with some of the fine accoutrements I've brought in from the city," stated the young merchant. He was humbled to find out that the city's merchants found no need for his garments. He left the shops, baffled.

He soon turned his gaze to the schoolhouse. "The impressionable minds of this town could do with some of my fine learning supplies," the young merchant stated. However, the teacher declined his pencils, inkwells, abaci, and rulers. The young merchant's confusion became disappointment. He reasoned that the refusal of his supplies was based on their ignorance.

He soon turned his gaze to the church. "The good saints of this town could use new Bibles and hymnals," stated the young merchant. However, the preachers found no use for his resources. He reasoned that the White folks in the city were students of the good book but Black folks loved theatrics. His disappointment grew to disgust.

The residents of this town rejected all his efforts. He could only conclude that these folks were simple with a sophisticated veneer. They hadn't quite evolved to recognize the utility of his offerings.

He even found the children to be peculiar. They played games that were foreign to him; however, he joined them in a nocturnal game. The young uns would seek out the darkest places in the woods. With only the faint light emanating from the moon, the pack would pick one unfortunate participant to be the Moon Man. The Moon Man would close his eyes and count to ten. Once he opened his eyes, he had only twenty seconds to give chase and capture a replacement. Twenty seconds was hardly enough time for his eyes to adjust to the utter darkness. This gave the others an advantage. Unfortunately, the young merchant was chosen to be that disadvantaged participant.

He let his eyes adjust, then gave chase. He repeated the routine more than he cared to. Their adolescent laughter and mockery spread through the woods. His counting grew more hasty and agitated. Soon his disgust turned to accusations. The young merchant's rage pierced the darkness as he cursed their activity. "This silly town would play a witless game!" He soon retired, determining to return home at the sun's first appearance.

The next morning he rose, ready to return to his city. As he waited for the train, he noticed a White couple beaming with excitement. He was compelled to learn about their interest in this town. Nothing intrigued him more than White people. Surely there was nothing in this city that could amuse people of their caliber. Although he studied them with great interest, he had not the courage to engage them before they engaged him. He decided that he would eavesdrop.

He heard the White couple raving about their time spent in the town. They loved the culture, the food, the music, and the hospitality of the people. They were sure that this city was unprecedented.

As soon as their praises landed on his ears, he felt a clutching in his chest that could only be described as his heart's attempt to reprimand the couple. He had never been more turned around in his life. He was scared of what would happen next. He was even more embarrassed at the thought of it happening in the presence of White people. He looked to the sky, and while he attempted to plead with God, the sun distracted him. He whispered with great contempt, "Even their sun is strange."

Although he got the last word, the city won the dispute. Even his last breaths mocked him, as he took them in the city he died loathing. The sun exposed his secret. This man's sky had a different sun.

There is much debate as to whether the incident really happened. Yet the tales of the Moon Man who died of a broken heart continue. A children's chorus tells of his death:

The Moon Man died; the Moon Man died.
His eyes can't find what the dark will hide.
Nothing dares grow where his body now lies.
The sun don't shine where the Moon Man died . . .

You should consider it the greatest of insults in this city to be called a Moon Man, Moonie, or Space Negro. Till this day there has not been one citizen who has dared to study astrology because of the off chance he or she would be called a Space Negro.

For the young merchant was indeed a Moon Man. He could not see. No matter how hard he tried, he could not adjust his sight when faced with things beyond his comprehension. The stories that formed his identity obstructed his view.

The young merchant did not know that the city boasted the best Negro schools. They had no need for his supplies, for they themselves are a supplier to many. The city's religious leaders are more traveled and learned than most of their fellows.

This city did not need the young merchant's approval. For he was not the first opponent, nor will he be the last. Many have tried to hustle the city, and many have been unsuccessful. For the city has endurance. It does not fatigue easily.

6

LIGHT WORDS IN A GOOD NIGHT

What I'm saying might be profane, but it's also profound.

—RICHARD PRYOR, *Pryor Convictions*

*T*his chapter will not be filled with side hugs and bashful temptations. When describing expressed anger, I will not use the words *freakin'*, *darn*, and *son of a gun*. This will not be PG-rated content. To be fair, the previous chapters haven't been *Afterschool Special* content. However, let me start with how not being PG caused bedlam with a Christian distributor and got my album removed from their bookstores and website.

In early 2017, my label at the time received an email stating that a major Christian retail chain would no longer carry my album because of complaints from customers. We were quickly informed that what had inspired the complaints was the use of the word *penis*.

In late 2016, I had released my fourth solo album, *The Narrative*. It was well received and landed in the top ten of hip-hop sales on iTunes the week of its release. Despite the general support and praise for the content, there seemed to be one song that rubbed consumers the wrong way. On the last song of the album, "Piano Break, 33 AD," I say,

> *I was an insecure boy who just thought he was a genius*
> *But always pissed off—that's because I thought with my*
> *penis*

The song is placed as the denouement of the album. My hope was to present this as my mountaintop speech before the march. Once all the evidence was laid out and the conversation had circled the room a few times, I wanted to present the conclusion of the matter: God is good! However, I found that others had a different interpretation of the song.

I was penalized by a religiously conservative institution for lamenting my personal sexual misconduct as a young man. No attention to context or room for nuance. If I'm honest, I'm not sure why my albums were in their stores to begin with—other than the sales, of course.

Once Bradford Davis published an article about the incident in the *Washington Post* in February 2017, I received emails from major publications and TV shows asking me to comment on the decision.

The *Washington Post* article created an upheaval that neither the distributor nor I expected. Not too long after the article hit the web, I was on the phone with their head of retail—the man who had made the decision to remove the album in the first place. If I was confused by their decision when they sent their initial email, I was more confused once I finished my call with the representative. He said that there seemed to be complaints about that lyric; however, he couldn't tell how many complaints nor give clarity about what process the company followed in these situations. He even stated that he found the lyric to be modest.

The *Washington Post* discovered that my album had been celebrated on the distributor's platform before the order to remove it: "His album 'The Narrative' . . . was once described with high praise on [the retailer's] product page as 'saturated in a Gospel worldview.'"[1]

How can an album that was labeled as "saturated in a Gospel worldview" become a liability within three months? Was it just marketing copy? Had no one bothered to actually listen to it? I mean, it *was*, of course. At least, before it fell victim to a hypocritical industry willing to be tossed to and fro by every opinion in order to sustain its bottom line. I pictured some mother out there, aghast: *How dare this young man talk about his penis and politics to my unblemished child!*

I record each track with great intentionality. I've censored myself on *many* occasions because of the context. Sometimes I feel that my intentions are impure or that I'm simply trying to be incendiary. At other times I censor myself for the benefit of the weaker ear. I would have never thought that the use of the word *penis* would make a vendor squeamish. The word is anatomically appropriate. The context was ethical and artful.

The real irony was that while they were fixated on the word *penis*, there were other words in there that I felt were more offensive. They missed a *bastard*, a *damn*, and a *hell naw*. But the more I've thought about it, the more I think that *penis* wasn't the real reason my album was removed. What I think was more threatening was my celebration of Black identity and my consistent chastising of White evangelical institutions and White supremacy in America. It was honest. But it was not comfortable.

I'm not the only person to have been banished from the chain. According to that same article in the *Washington Post,* the late author Rachel Held Evans was also banned for using the anatomical word *vagina*. Rather than our language, I believe it was our theology that was considered inappropriate.

How can people bothered by these words esteem a Bible that contains the Song of Solomon? In high school I plagiarized a chapter of that biblical book in a love letter I gave to my girlfriend. She thought I was the freakiest (and most poetic) young man to ever explore the English language. Those are words intended to make a person blush.

We must ask ourselves how we got here. Conservative Christians and sanctified saints have lost many cultural battles over the twentieth century. The religious ricochet of the Scopes Trial, southern animosity toward civil rights, and the sexual revolution each changed how the traditional Christian community engaged culture. But rather than adapting and preaching on "the unknown god" as Paul did, many Christians preferred to create their own insular gated communities. To sculpt their own small and inoffensive statues. The farther you move from the flames, the harder it is to discern heat. Cultural distance has made us Christians cold and stiff.

Humans are moved by our fleshly impulses to engage in the vilest of activities. There's a reason the Bible prohibits bestiality. Human depravity led someone to engage in that act. The Bible is not ignorant about our desires and how they move us to act in ways that violate the image of God in us, to use our ability to work and create for chaos instead of holiness. But if the Bible is honest about our brokenness, then what makes us think that we should edit the direct or even the obscene in our redemptive narratives? Just to choose one example, the practice of ignoring healthy conversations around sexuality has made many Christians either too volatile in discourse, too intimidated to engage, or prone to being bullied into affirming the spectrum of sexual identities.

Surely there's an alternative?

Surely it includes being able to speak freely?

Surely?

At what point does separation from the world become more dangerous than beneficial? Many Christians today have bloomed in artificial light. They have no comprehension of the dark. Their eyes have not adjusted.

One of the greatest areas of neglect in our churches is that we fail to understand that even though the sun creates shadows, there's no place the sun can't reach. Jesus exposed the thoughts of the Pharisees. He replayed the past of the woman at the well. He looked into the future of Peter. There is no vault where we can hide our most hideous secrets from Jesus. It amuses me that Christians come to the faith admitting their brokenness and sinful ways but eventually get to the place where they abandon that honesty.

Darkness is not always opaque, and light is not always safe. We can learn much from observing an obscene world. An abundance of either dark or light hinders our ability to function. And, with all we've seen already about creating from a place of honesty, how will our work ever change the world if we can't see it and say it like it is?

When you walk into a dark room, it takes time for your eyes to adjust. The slightest bit of moonlight slanting into the room will help you. However, complete darkness is a playground for fools. If we never let light into the darkest places of our hearts and culture, our eyes will never have a chance to adjust. We will remain in a state of perpetual adolescence.

Light seems harmless. But the Christian art community's propensity to censor itself impairs our ability to discern the borders of the pure and the profane. To sit in a room with blinding lights would create the same impairment as a pitch-black cave. Too much light keeps you from seeing.

The goal is not to fetishize the obscene but to be honest and accurate. In a small gathering I once attended, I heard actor Mykelti Williamson, of *Forrest Gump* and *Fences* fame, speak about mentoring a young actor in the role of a deplorable gangster. The young actor had reservations about playing a character of low morals. He couldn't find much reason to accept the role. Williamson explained that his responsibility was to play the character in such a way that the audience would leave the theater disgusted. Although Hollywood does a wonderful job of romanticizing depravity, I still find this statement to be true. Honestly show us the darkest parts of our souls, and we will beg for the light. You will have made this world a little truer. A little better.

Portraying this individual in an honest way is an act of redemption. Give detail to the edges. Show the cracks without romanticizing them. Paint his nihilistic destruction. Let the crowd see corruption for what it is—a ravenous creature that will devour its surroundings, then refuse to spare its own carcass.

What is grotesque, obscene, or dark is not always evil. These characteristics are simply eggs ready to be cracked to reveal truth.

The novelist Flannery O'Connor had a pen that lived among derelicts and an imagination that lodged in the most grotesque of motels. However, her fiction delivers truth and comfort, even though it's set in surroundings that are foreign to the majority of Christian art today.

This style conveyed what O'Connor and other students of Henry James referred to as the "felt life."[2] Writers were to submerge themselves in their environment and see it *all* as beautiful.

O'Connor gave instruction on how to discern the

depraved: "To be able to recognize a freak, you have to have some conception of the whole man."[3] This is not just about what makes a freak but about what makes a saint and how both can exist in the same space. Her ability to hold beauty and suffering was most likely fueled by her own struggle with lupus, a disease that eventually proved fatal.

Even more concerning to many Christians is the ability of writers like O'Connor to be honest about the world without feeling compelled to race through the rough stuff to a nice benediction.

When we edit the legitimate horror and vulgarity from our world, we also edit the real redemption and empathy that wait on the other side. When our storytelling has generic evil, the resulting deliverance is about as interesting as tax law. O'Connor did a masterful job of dealing with the dysfunction of society. Her characters are honest and complex. I find myself more intrigued by the "naive" racism of Tanner in "Judgement Day" than the pristine ensemble of characters we often find in Christian art.

When narratives are void of the true and horrific, we prepare people for a disturbing experience of the world. Reality is not kind to those unused to it. I don't advocate for all our art to be realism. However, I'm always concerned when an overwhelming amount of our art misses a golden opportunity.

Scripture portrays a caravan of saints and savages. It delivers words that inspire praise and panic. Although free of expletives and mockery, Ecclesiastes 7 stands in opposition to today's glossy art:

The day you die is better than the day you are born.
Better to spend your time at funerals than at parties.
>   After all, everyone dies—
>   so the living should take this to heart.
Sorrow is better than laughter,
>   for sadness has a refining influence on us.
A wise person thinks a lot about death,
>   while a fool thinks only about having a good
>   time.[4]

This text should be an ever-present hum in our ears. The Author is telling us to have both death and life on our minds. My pastor friend Darryl Ford once gave greater context to this passage on my podcast: "Sometimes celebration becomes a form of escapism from the mourning that God says is actually good for us."[5]

A movement will always draw controversy. For example, in the midst of Black Lives Matter protests, it doesn't take much effort to find dissenters who believe that concern over police brutality is baseless. They are often quick to distract from the point—to mention criminal records or improper responses to police authority. But why should that keep us from wondering why these horrendous acts are happening?

Evangelical exceptionalism often hypocritically implies that grace is afforded only to those who are without error.

If this is the case, then heaven will be vacant.

Truly creative Christians see the range of human emotions as something to explore without restrictions. I want that for all my brothers and sisters. We fear sin so much that we are willing to lock out wisdom. We don't trust ourselves with the unedited canon of human experience; therefore, we keep others from it. This never leads to the best results socially or artistically. In terms of a story, our characters become flat and predictable. There is nothing impressive about their victories. Life is a slam dunk when you're living with low goals. And since when have those changed anything for the better?

Where there is raw human rage and anger, might not we hear *fuck, shit,* or *damn*? Where there is love or lust, should we look away from the human reality of sex? Where there is hatred, isn't the reality of stinging insults, epithets, and slurs something with which we must grapple? Where there is immorality, must not the raw result—violence, rape, and crime—be honestly evaluated?

I recognize that this is not everyone's life, but is this not an accurate representation of our world? Is our God so prudish that he is not aware of these aspects of it? Does he cover his face with embarrassment? Is his eye only on the sparrow? Who reports the heinous news to him? If God is unaware, then he is an irresponsible Lord. And if we ignore these realities, we are irresponsible artists. I believe the artist must take these risks. These risks can be triggers, but they can also heal. Do you know these emotions?

What makes a word inappropriate? Three years before *The Narrative,* I released an album called *Talented 10th.* That album was also considered for removal from Christian distribution. It features a song called "Chapter 9: Jim

Crow." In it I addressed the racial tension I felt was being ignored in many Christian spaces:

> *They gave me a slave pen for my freedom of speech*
> *Yeah, I'm trying to leave the island but swimming through*
> *bleach . . .*

> *Miseducate, colonize, divide*
> *Teach beauty is straight hair and the bluest of eyes . . .*

> *How a privileged man gon' say it's time to move forward*
> *And say the game's fair when he monopolizes the board?*

These lyrics were celebrated by many, but they stung others. However, most of the backlash came from my use of other strong words:

> *I guess I'm stuck here on Nigga Island*
> *Where niggas be wylin' and color is violence*
> *Moment of silence . . .*

> *That lady you call ho, that's my lover*
> *That woman you call bitch, that's my mother*

Many moons have passed since hip-hop artists have needed to defend themselves for the use of such words. I recognize I'm no regular artist. These words were used with prudence and intentionality. But I calculated the cost, and I knew that, in order to talk about racism and misogyny in an authentic way, I needed to use the right language for the context. Many found it to be tasteless and unnecessary. Some believe certain words are outside the reach of redemption. I am not one of those people.

I am not for searing one's conscience or crossing personal boundaries. But neither do I believe we can place personal restrictions on the gospel. "Christian" stories that skip the rawness of human life simply to get to the grace-filled ending miss out on a grand opportunity to spotlight human weakness. In films like *The Blind Side* or *The Grace Card* (which I acted in), stories that should have held extreme racial tension instead glossed over it with elementary insults that misdiagnosed the sickness in the world.

Christian art does not need porcelain icons. Sure, they're appealing, but they break with the slightest tension. The Spirit of God has made us into precious gems who can endure the pressures of life. Beautiful but strong. If our call is to be salt in the world, then we must be honest about the sanctified and the scandalous.

Every community is depraved beneath its veneer. Some communities and households put their brokenness on display through homelessness, gang violence, and drug addiction. But how many other communities hide similar dysfunction behind posh homes and fancy clothes?

Some are afraid of the dark. Others are entangled by it. The more we sanitize the world, the more likely we are to be traumatized by its evil. We should never be callous to evil, but we should never be shocked. We should be appalled and outraged. But our righteous indignation always comes with control and austerity.

Our art replicates either the shallowness or the depth of our relationships with God and people. If, when we gather in accountability circles, our most arduous fight is against socially acceptable sins like pride or procrastination, then haven't we lied to God and ourselves? We're ashamed to confess violent thoughts, lustful desires, prejudices, and the depth of our selfish inclinations. It's possible that I'm the chief of sinners like Paul and stand as the lone Christian among sinners. Or might Christian culture have created groups of perpetual liars?

This is not solely the fault of the individual. Our institutions struggle with honesty and often promote shame. The more grotesque the sinner, the deeper that person falls into Dante's inferno. We say all sin is offensive before a holy God, but all the time, we're evaluating based on a complex hierarchy of socially acceptable wrongs. I definitely believe that some sins have greater impact on society. But I don't believe that any act is beyond redemption. Our narratives should reflect that.

When I first came to the faith, my main concern was to abstain from sexual immorality, drug use, and fits of rage. I was blessed to have a brother who quickly aided me in my spiritual formation. I began to develop tools and practices that made me a better believer, friend, and citizen. I would soon learn that the Christian faith is about much more than avoiding sin. As my brother Dhati would say, "It's about growing in devotion, love, and service to God and others." Jesus didn't die just for us to avoid sin and flee temptation. He also died for us to push back darkness and to walk among the grotesque.

At one point I believed I could no longer love the films I once watched. My pure eyes could not handle the darkness of the world. At that point I didn't know how to reconcile the things I knew to be good from my old life with this new worldview I had. If you are this person, I would encourage you to feel affirmed in your decision to flee temptation. It's best to keep away from the dark if you know you have the propensity to stumble. However, I feel there are many of us whose eyes have adjusted to engage such situations.

Brace yourself. The truth is that HBO's *The Wire* taught me more about the interconnectedness of corrupt human civilization than many well-written Christian articles. That television show helped me gain empathy even as I've dealt with drug abuse and violence in close proximity to me. The exhaustion of a young Michael B. Jordan's Wallace as he attempts to escape the drug life only to be murdered by a friend painted a picture of depravity more lasting than many sermons I've heard. My brother Reggie's fight with drug addiction, which led to his redemption and return to family and faith, is no easy story to tell and would probably be too raw for the Christian film industry.

Rather than having reading groups that pass around tired ideas about missions, maybe small group leaders should pass out box sets of *The Wire* to soften the hearts of discerning church members. *The Wire* painted dignity and depravity, gold and shadow. The show left subtle portraits for us to wrestle with. One dark night, a young child sits on his front stoop, surrounded by the sounds of an active city, because that gives him more respite than being inside his home. That is an image that stays with you.

But *The Wire* wasn't restricted to pain and the grotesque. It also celebrated the joys that real people feel. Many Christian stories have shallow losses, which means they have shallow victories.

But, of course, the reverse is true too. I'm often amused by secular films that cover religion and religious people. Where Christian art misses out on properly detailing the dark, mainstream cinema misfires on the beauty and utility of our Christian faith. Christians are often sculpted as one-dimensional stoics who carry about as much joy as a dying plant.

If you watch films like *Sister Act, Footloose, Let It Shine,* or *But I'm a Cheerleader,* you will get the same recycled religious characters. Christians are hardly ever portrayed as nuanced or just. They are usually won over to the opposing side or subjectively stubborn. Not only can secular films misdiagnose the foundational dysfunction in human relationships; they also fail to see how the church heals those broken relationships. They lose the gold in the shadows.

In the film *The Dark Knight Rises,* the character Bane explains to Batman why he will not succeed in his attempt to fight in the dark. In his smothered thick accent, Bane calmly informs Batman, "You merely adopted the dark. I was born in it, molded by it."[6]

In that film, in order for the hero to overcome the

villain, he has to embrace aspects of the dark that were intimidating to him. It shows a powerful truth—there is a difference between embracing the dark and submitting to it.

If you want to have a missionary's heart, don't hide from all things obscene. Receive the prayer that Jesus prayed for his disciples in John 17—that the Father would protect us from the Evil One—while at the same time honestly acknowledging that we can never evade the presence of evil:

> I am not praying that you take them out of the
> world but that you protect them from the evil one.
> They are not of the world, just as I am not of the
> world. Sanctify them by the truth; your word is
> truth. As you sent me into the world, I also have
> sent them into the world.[7]

In this passage, Jesus revealed that our best protection from the world is not isolation but the truth of God. This will sanctify us. This will protect us.

Be equipped with the Word and go into the world. Keeping ourselves from the darkness of the world will not make us adequate missionaries for the kingdom.

When I became a Christian, I began to frequent men's groups where we would often play basketball. I truly enjoyed those moments. However, many of these pickup scenarios and church leagues were the epitome of Christian fragility. Men who had once played basketball with passion and drive were now soft and indecisive on the court. I felt that they were holding back. It was as if the Monstars of *Space Jam* had zapped the athleticism from them. I wholeheartedly accept that our faith makes us more compassionate and sensitive, but it doesn't remove our excellence or our drive.

But often we mistake passion for idolatry. Christians should be sensitive to how things affect their character. We should always ask ourselves, *Does this thing own me? Can I live without it?* Sometimes our fear of engaging the dark world isn't our fear of sin and our desire to be sanctified from the obscene; it's our fear of being among people who are willing to excel in a space at any cost. Without selling their souls, Christians should be as passionate about excelling.

I would be lying if I said that I didn't find my competition in Christian creative spaces less intimidating than mainstream spaces. If I'm not careful, I can become complacent in my work. The goal isn't to be the best. The goal is to be honest. Honesty will lead to excellence. If we remain siloed, we will never know the power of our work or the power of the gospel.

The truth of God makes us new. It gives us new joys. We should celebrate these new gifts each morning like children on Christmas. However, let's not lose that sense of familiarity that keeps us close to the people. The gospel redeems and reforms, but it doesn't remove our compassion and awareness of the darkness in this world. Contrary to the belief of many, sanctification doesn't remove this familiarity. According to Romans 12, rather than forgetting and forsaking, we are being reshaped for reentry. Although, like Bane, we were molded in the dark, each of us has been redeemed into a Batman who can use it for liberation and redemption.

In a present-COVID-19 world, many people are becoming more knowledgeable about viruses and vaccines. In the early part of the 2020 pandemic, I spoke with infectious-disease specialist and assistant professor of biomedical engineering at the University of Florida, Dr. Ivana Parker, about the various strategies within vaccine development. "Vaccines can incorporate proteins from viral or bacterial pathogens known to mount an immune response," she told me. "Exposure to altered pathogens in these ways allows the body a chance to develop and strengthen specific immune responses so that when exposed to live bacterial or viral threats, there can be a quick and robust response—to prevent the development of disease."[8]

There's a principle here. Although the virus of evil is active and exposure is highly likely, the gospel acts as a vaccine that weakens the power of the darkness, and it can keep us safe from the ultimate danger of death. However, it requires a daily dose. We must be wise and discerning without believing we have to isolate ourselves from the world. I would have been a better leader if I hadn't thought that renewing my mind meant removing myself from the world.

Let me offer this caveat: vulnerable souls do need shelter. As one example, sometimes families should keep their kids and themselves from content that can infect pure hearts and minds. There is possibly nothing more damaging to children than exposing them to perverted human behaviors.

But kids grow. And what is healthy changes as we change. In many churches we use pizza, cool music, and funny skits to distract teenagers from the many things they desire to explore. Instead of teaching young men and women how to understand and address their appetites, we teach them to ignore those appetites. In doing so, we are only creating sexual aggression toward the church. Would we rather these kids learn the intimate nuances of sex from people who thrive on perversion and sensationalism or from those who should understand the difference between the beneficial and the profane? One extreme teaches sexual repression and wonders why many become sexually defiant. Another extreme teaches sexual relativism and wonders why many are concerned about changes in society.

We risk warping our children's sense of good and evil when we paint evil with a dark aesthetic and good with a glossy tint. We know these tropes fall short of the real faces of good and evil. Evil rarely looks identifiable. It doesn't walk around with an eye patch and black trench coat. The home where it rests its head isn't always a suffocating dungeon absent of light.

Sometimes evil is attractive. Jim Jones was an enticing preacher. Ted Bundy was a charming man. Idi Amin was a popular politician. Sometimes evil is dressed in light. Sometimes evil wins. That doesn't remove its stench.

Are we being honest? Or are we creating fragile Christians who don't know how to handle obstacles and pain? When they experience these things, they end up thinking the church was a liar the whole time.

This is the posture of Philip Pullman's novel series His Dark Materials. Pullman positioned "the Church" as an institution with a sinister plot to keep others from experiencing the liberation of their true selves. There is no grand sinister plan afoot in the real world, but the assessment rings true on a micro level. It benefits institutions to have their members turn to them for all needs. Companies do this as well. It's a distorted reach for power and authority. Apple makes sure there is little chance you can get service for their products apart from them. Their frequent updates and changes feel more like reminders of authority than genuine upgrades. It benefits the company's brand to control all that orbits around them.

The church in many ways has sought this control by censoring our words and thoughts. Of course, this is not true of all churches—maybe not even most. But it's true of many. Enough to shape a culture. If congregants are clueless about the world or constantly persuaded to avoid it, then they will continue to seek unnecessary counsel from church authorities. We removed the need for the Holy Spirit to intercede.

There's a difference between being a realist and being a pessimist. There's a difference between discerning in the darkness and dealing in dysfunction. There is no need to praise the dark, but there is a need to praise in it. There's a difference between observation and celebration. It's Rembrandt's *Danae* versus Hefner's *Playboy*. It's John Mayer's "Gravity" versus Amy Winehouse's "Rehab." It's the depiction of violence in *The Passion of the Christ* versus its depiction in the *Saw* films.

Clean art can be misleading and filled with a poisonous positivism. Obscene art can be fraudulent with its depiction of nihilism. The gross betrayal in the garden catalyzed the grand display of God's grace. As O'Connor knew, the grotesque is necessary for us to identify the image of God.

We are residents of a kingdom that is not of this world but still in it. We do not rejoice in violence, sexual sin, and lawlessness. However, our kingdom is reached by a narrow road that welcomes the dishonorable to new citizenship. We do not forget the lives we lived and the struggles we still have.

However, to know the dark and not be overcome by it is to walk in real victory and courage. Not a baseless arrogance that ignores the dangers but a courage that sees the fiery darts cutting through the air and knows how to avoid their sting. It's the courage that Christ transferred to us after declaring that all authority is his. We have this courage in earthen vessels, but we are not easily broken.

The holy Scriptures are genuine and profitable because of their engagement with the dark and grotesque. The vengeance portrayed could fill the heart of Grendel's mother in *Beowulf*. The sexual exploitation rivals *The Bluest Eye*. Violence paints the pages like *Game of Thrones*. Treachery moves through the narrative like Iago, and its mystery trumps the world of Macondo. The Bible describes the most heinous act in human history, which was the audacity of humans to think they could kill God and rest well. Their prayers were just light words in a good night.

Both beauty and horror can be discovered at the manger as well as at the foot of the cross. If we know Scripture to be true, then God has ordained all things for our good,[9] and the telling of "all things" must be for our good as well. Stories of either happiness or despair can be liberating. There is both beauty and truth in Yahweh's creation and destruction.

I become excited when I discover Christians who can journey into the dark. They explore it not because they are intoxicated by it. They know that exploration is necessary in order to show how big our God is. There is no obscenity that makes him blush. There is no sin that catches him off guard.

Are we brave enough to believe that?

MYHOOD, USA, 1931

Once upon a time not long ago
Before the civil rights movement and the new Jim
   Crow:
Sit back—I'll introduce you to a wonderful place
In every state, called Myhood, USA.
Life wasn't perfect, but folks did what they could;
These people took pride in their neighborhood.
They had doctors and lawyers, artists, barbers, and
   teachers,
Entrepreneurs, politicians, and preachers.

They had stable universities, sports teams, and
   banks.
You invest and trade here 'cause in other places you
   can't.
It was Black owned from the cradle to the coffin—
Before the NBA, we had a history of ballin'.
It was Durham, Greenwood, Atlanta's Sweet Auburn,
Quakertown in Denton, Third Ward, Houston. But here
   a caution:
While some wanted their turn to earn and make a
   living,
Some just wanted them to burn, baby, burn—it was
   vicious.

If the city wasn't bombed or maybe destroyed by
   flames,

It eventually changed because of eminent domain.
How can you own a home if you can't get a loan
And the powers that be could redline your zone?
The government wants your value to drop;
Then the private investors come through and buy up
    your spot.
You can't win fighting the government and KKK.
Plus, integration hurt Myhood in a curious way.

Black moved to the burbs, trying to escape the
    system,
But they took stability and wealth right along with
    them.
With no ownership and financial stimulation,
It makes it much easier for gentrification.
They don't build schools to build wealth, to build
    wisdom,
So instead, we build debt, and they build more
    prisons.
With few taxpayers, they make money off policing:
Fines and tickets—I'm getting searched for no
    reason.

Police are underpaid, but they are making a killing.
And compound that with the crack epidemic,
So now we got dope fiends shootin' dope
Who don't know the meaning of Harvard nor hope,
Howard, FAMU, even Tuskegee,
Morehouse, next to the poorhouse. Baby, we leaving,
For the American dream, it's in burbs now.
Opportunities in Myhood get turned down.

Community service groups turn into gangs.
They're hammers with bad aim; they bangin' on
    everything.
So now my friend on the next street becomes my
    enemy—
No jobs to distract us, 'cause we don't have an industry.
All they have are liquor stores next to a Burger King,
Next to a pawn shop, next to a Dairy Queen,
Next to a Chinese store, next to a gas station,
Next to the five churches, next to the building that's
    vacant.
Most of the businesses are owned by Asians,
So money never stays in the same location.
This is truth; this ain't hating.
If the church can't change, then who should we place
    faith in?
Some blame welfare, and some blame the music.
Some blame the dealer, and some blame the user.
Turn on the news—let's figure out who we're blaming.
Many benefit off Myhood not changing.

Exploit my culture they're aiding and abetting.
It's the Black stock exchange they're buying and
    selling.
A generation of self-hate and psychosis—
In Myhood it's almost innate to feel hopeless.
Predatory lending and banking in Myhood—
We ain't creating wealth; we just importing goods.
"A change gon' come" is what I tell the youngster.
This is a love song; I like to call it "Justice."

7

YOU GOOD?

Now all has been heard;
here is the conclusion of the matter:
Fear God and keep his commandments,
for this is the duty of all mankind.

—ECCLESIASTES 12:13, NIV

Who knew that the Lord could be so good?

I mean, the church people told me, but I didn't listen. They sang, but it never reached my ears. They danced, but I never seemed to catch the rhythm. They knew something I didn't.

I didn't feel him. I had no taste. I was feasting off another's plate. I drank deficient gospels and sniffed the fading aroma of factions. But now I have ears to hear, eyes to see, and hands to feel. And when my feet fail me, he is standing there with hands extended, ready to continue the dance. He is a good God who gives good gifts.

My friend, we've been given every spiritual gift to be effective for the kingdom. To make this place look like

Eden with the gifts of our good work. There is no good thing that God keeps from us. We often get in our own way. We allow our own restrictions to keep us from seeing the full painting. Others have tried to paint God for us, and they have painted an insufferable God.

He is not just a God to study; he is a God to feel. When he gets into your toes, you jump with more joy. When he gets into your hands, you craft with more care. When he gets into your lungs, you speak with more love. Your senses are heightened, and the fire is in your bones. Do you feel it?

I first heard the gospel message preached as a young man. I see now that I was intrigued by Jesus because I was afraid of hell. But as I've matured, I've been drawn to Jesus because of much more than my desire to escape from the consequences of sin. Yes, I'm grateful to no end that I'm free from the ultimate consequence of an eternity without God. However, I find Christianity even more compelling because of its beneficial worldview. It keeps me motivated to operate in a world of corrupted ideas, systems, and people in need of heavenly hope.

Once my faith took on flesh and walked within me, I could see it work and live. I had the theological imagination to see how my creative life would be a blessing to the world. I could feel a good God who gives good gifts.

This book has been mostly musings about people, events, movements, and ideas that I believe could help us cultivate good work and creativity. Now let me provide you with seven principles that will move you closer to a blessed creative life—yes, one that can repair a broken world.

Romans 12:1–2 sets up how to capture our redemptive identity and calling:

> Brothers and sisters, in view of the mercies of God, I urge you to present your bodies as a living sacrifice, holy and pleasing to God; this is your true worship. Do not be conformed to this age, but be transformed by the renewing of your mind, so that you may discern what is the good, pleasing, and perfect will of God.[1]

Before we can be effective in engagement, we must present our bodies (work, calling, and gifts) as sacrifices. They do not belong to us; therefore, we should be wise but not miserly with them.

Also, we must consider that the very act of sacrificial living is our true form of worship. It's not just the singing of songs and the bending of knees. What good are our prayers if we're selfish and self-indulgent once we stand up and begin to walk?

The practice of daily sacrifice will keep our minds from being enticed by the philosophies of the world. These habits will cultivate great discernment that will be a blessing to you and our Father in heaven.

There is no one I find who captures the essence of the seven essentials more than the legendary George Washington Carver.

George Washington Carver was born into slavery in Missouri. His father died shortly after he was born, and his mother was murdered when she and George were kidnapped. Eventually his slave owner tracked George down and returned him to his plantation.

As a young child, Carver was constantly sick. Because of his lack of physical strength, he spent most of his time in fields, growing his affection for plants, science, and painting nature. Carver felt an intrinsic connection to nature and said, "Many are the tears I have shed because I would break the roots or flower off of some of my pets while removing them from the ground."[2]

Around the farm, Carver quickly took on the moniker "the plant doctor." He went on to become a biologist, painter, and professor. It has been documented that he developed over four hundred products from legumes and sweet potatoes. He credited these discoveries to an uncanny practice: "I found that when I talk to the little flower or little peanut it will give up its secrets."[3]

George Washington Carver was highly sought after for his mind and products. Booker T. Washington hired him to oversee the agriculture department at Tuskegee Institute. Indian activist Mahatma Gandhi sought dietary advice from Carver in regard to his hunger strikes. President Franklin Delano Roosevelt used Carver's oil massage therapies for his polio. Inventors Henry Ford and Thomas Edison both offered jobs to the incomparable Carver.

Even the arrogant, simpleminded leaders of the racist

South couldn't ignore Carver's brilliance, and they sought his ingenuity to save the southern economy by encouraging farmers to grow crops that would be better for the soil.

Although Carver had hundreds of inventions, he never patented any of them. He was truly generous with his talent and treasure. He shared his ideas and methods with all, stating, "I didn't make these discoveries. God has only worked through me to reveal to his children some of his wonderful providence."[4]

Glenn Clark shared one man's life-changing experience of meeting Carver in his book *The Man Who Talks with the Flowers*:

> I went to the lecture expecting to learn science and came away knowing more about prayer than I had ever learned in the theological schools.[5]

If we're looking for validation of personal formation that happens outside the typical restrictions, then Carver gives us ample reason to become students of that kind of formation.

Carver embraced this unconventional formation. He felt God in a tangible way:

> Reading about nature is fine, but if a person walks in the woods and listens carefully, he can learn more than what is in books, for they speak with the voice of God.[6]

Carver's faith may seem like senseless spirituality or pantheism. However, this is the type of theology formed on the plantations and outside the stiff halls of academia. It's just the type of story you'd find between dry bones walking and Jesus walking on water. It's the type of intimacy that people have with God when they're called to a creative life beyond the reproduction of trite systems in seminaries.

How can we place ourselves in the position to feel the real presence of God while we serve others? Here are seven essentials of effective engagement.

1. Reject Idols (Including Yourself)

Creatives—and those who spend their lives implementing creative solutions—have the power to illuminate ideas and draw others' eyes to particular products. We can use our gifts for blessing or manipulation. We can be chiefs that obstruct the view of our tribes, or we can lead in a way that reminds others of the grace and authority of Yahweh.

There is nothing more intoxicating than the applause and praise of humans. It's a high that can last a lifetime. Many of us are in our careers because someone told us that we were good and we believed that person. Affirmation is powerful. However, it can also be a curse. The unintended consequence of being good in your work is that it draws people to adore you. How you handle that affection is of paramount importance. Either you can appreciate it and be sober minded, or you can be preoccupied living for the approval of people. Let's not paint false images that distract viewers from the true masterpiece.

To be great in our work is to be humble. Romans 12:3 gives a reason:

> By the grace given to me, I tell everyone among you
> not to think of himself more highly than he should
> think. Instead, think sensibly, as God has distrib-
> uted a measure of faith to each one.[7]

We must constantly remind ourselves that we can go
from Eden's honest orphans to thieves who desire to steal
the show. Humility is crucial. Just as we don't want to be
idols that obstruct others' view of God, we don't want the
things we do to eclipse the God for whom we do them.

We can easily overestimate our role in the kingdom.
We accept our place as tools being used; then we gradually
try to become the hand that uses the tools. I'm reminded
of the swift rebuke given to the priest visiting heaven in
C. S. Lewis's *The Great Divorce*. The clergyman wants a
guarantee that his work will be important there, but he is
gently rebuked:

> I can promise you none of these things. No sphere
> of usefulness: you are not needed there at all. No
> scope for your talents: only forgiveness for having
> perverted them.[8]

When we don't control our lives and work, they control
us. When we are no longer being transformed by the renewing of our minds, we become worshippers of our work.

Even when our work doesn't carry an overt message, it
still has a purpose. In the past I used the maxim "Art for
art's sake." I typically meant that art shouldn't be tethered
to a purpose. My view has changed. Our art may not be
tethered to an *outcome*, but it always has a *purpose* whether

we recognize it or not. We are worshipping through our creation. We are speaking a fundamental truth about our nature and the nature of elements we use. We are demonstrating dominion that was given to us by God. Our creativity is not chaotic and baseless. It conveys truth about the world God designed. Jackson Pollock's abstract expressionism and Ernie Barnes's ghetto dramatizations present two different truths about the world.

Let's not spurn the Giver for the gifts that he gives.

2. Join with Others for Others

It's of uttermost importance that we understand that all gifts God gives us are for the benefit of *others*. Romans 12:4–5 lets us know that we are part of a great community and each individual has value:

> As in one body we have many members, and the members do not all have the same function, so we, though many, are one body in Christ, and individually members one of another.

It's easy to think that whatever role you play has less value than others. We've been conditioned to think that those who work in full-time ministry positions land higher on God's priority list. This is a lie that has damaged many lives and relationships. This hierarchy has created a lust for talents that are used most frequently in the church. The individual who shows hospitality is hardly praised as much as the one who sings. However, who wants to listen to a beautiful voice in a cold and unwelcoming environment? We need one another.

Paul lets us know that all gifts are important, and many of those gifts will be used outside church gatherings. We must recognize our need for community.

The Bible has dozens of "one another" commands. Essentially, the Scriptures are telling us that it is impossible to please God outside of loving the "other." We can't even claim to love God if we don't love our brother.

Supporting and serving others keeps us honest with our gifts. We serve others not only when it benefits us but also when it's most risky. What is love when it's safe? We should always be willing to give our platform to those who have proven to be faithful and genuine with their gifts. The stage is not ours to dominate. There's nothing worse than insecure people who are intimidated by other talented people. If we believe God is a giver of good gifts, we surely can't believe that we're the only ones to be blessed by his generosity. We are to emulate that generosity.

We must also be vigilant in training others. The discipleship process has been mismanaged in many Christian spaces. Although it's useful to practice one-on-one mentorship, it's quite important that we don't lose sight of the importance of community. Too often we think of training individuals as a solo project. Jesus could do that because he had every spiritual gift to pass down. We are extremely limited people who can give only the best of ourselves, which will still leave quite a deficiency in the mentee. The only way we can fill the gap is by multiple people contributing to the growth of that individual. Growth is a *we* activity, not an *I* activity.

3. Find the Dignity in Difference

While we are a diverse nation that seems to endorse diversity, we must learn the difference between appreciation and appropriation or even exploitation. It is very important that we learn to celebrate and honor diversity and not manipulate the exchanges that happen in cross-cultural and cross-racial relationships. We must destroy the spiritual caste systems constructed around us.

In Mark 9, we find the disciples of Jesus arguing about who was the greatest. Jesus reproached them: "If anyone would be first, he must be last of all and servant of all."[9]

At times we are all jealous disciples who need to be checked about our place in the kingdom. Our work and skills can often make us feel loftier than we should.

Romans 12:5–8 exhorts us to find room for others:

> We, though many, are one body in Christ, and individually members one of another. Having gifts that differ according to the grace given to us, let us use them: if prophecy, in proportion to our faith; if service, in our serving; the one who teaches, in his teaching; the one who exhorts, in his exhortation; the one who contributes, in generosity; the one who leads, with zeal; the one who does acts of mercy, with cheerfulness.

What is worse than open neglect is the poisonous dishonor we conceal while thinking we look like we appreciate differences. In Spike Lee's 1989 film, *Do the Right Thing,* Lee's character Mookie is talking to his coworker

Pino (played by John Turturro) about his racist language. Mookie runs down a list of Pino's favorite celebrities and athletes. This list includes Prince, Eddie Murphy, and Michael Jordan. Mookie is exposing the harsh truth that even though Pino constantly calls Black people "nigger," all his favorite celebrities and athletes are "niggers." "They're different," Pino replies. Pino has deceived himself. He has created a narrative that separates Black performance from the dignity the person deserves. As long as these people were talented and could entertain him, they were worth appreciation. However, if they couldn't serve in that way, they were of no value.[10]

This type of thinking has plagued American society since its creation. Slaves were valued for entertainment but not considered worthy of freedom. Black entertainers in Hollywood and Harlem could dance and sing on the same stages as White folks, but they couldn't sleep in the same hotels.

Many of us manage our language much better than Pino, but our actions show us to be people who can appropriate all the fine things from a culture without truly caring about that culture's pain.

There is no dignity in honoring what people can do without honoring the people themselves. The exploitation of gifts has been a problem in the church too. Leaders use the talents of members for their own agendas. As leaders in this space, they must understand how to serve the greater community, not just themselves.

Neither should artists and others appropriate the church for their own benefit without giving any true commitment to the community that they are called to love and honor.

4. Repent and Repair

If you've seen a Marvel movie in the last decade, then you should be familiar with Iron Man. Iron Man is the creation of the fictional charismatic genius Tony Stark. Iron Man flies around the world, saving lives and restoring peace where there is chaos. Tony Stark created all the problems Iron Man has to solve. If you've watched any of his movies, you've seen how Stark created unnecessary dangers that come back to haunt him—warlords, artificial intelligence, and scorned archenemies.

If Tony Stark had greater compassion for others and a better theology of work, he would have less of a need to fly around the world, saving lives. His convictions would stop him before disaster loomed.

If we are honest, this is an indictment of many in the church. Monday through Friday, we are causing chaos through our vocations, politics, and actions, but then we want to throw on a cape, do missions, and save the world. If we just did better work, we would avoid a lot of problems. It's a blessing to find Christians who are willing to repent of wrongdoing and make amends; however, what better testimony is it to watch your step before you crush the neck of your sister?

To see properly, we must engage in daily introspection and renewal. This may require us to answer some hard questions about ourselves and our work. It would be naive for us to think that everything we put our hands to is blessing those around us. Oftentimes we are on the wrong side of justice. Once you scrutinize yourself and your contributions, you may have to repent and repair the damage.

Repentance is not some tame acknowledgment of wrongdoing. It's a sincere and aggressive redirection on the part of the offender. Repentance and repair are necessary in order for there to be harmony as we engage one another.

The preaching of repentance and repair is not for the weak. It stands in the face of ignorance and power and speaks unadulterated truth. Reconciliation without truth is flattery that will be easily broken. No relationship can be built on a foundation of unrepentance. This is a truth that brings many in America to recognize its need to repair the damage it created during slavery.

The Christian participates in the reconciliation of all things to God. We don't have the luxury of avoiding this. This means people, systems, and activities. Romans 12:14 gives instructions that are very difficult to swallow: "Bless those who persecute you; bless and do not curse them." This is the type of belief that makes our work otherworldly. This is the type of mindset that can be threatened night after night with phone calls and bombs, yet you wake up each day to preach a nonviolent message of hope and love. These are not easy instructions, but our God gives good gifts and commands.

The story of a Swedish chemist's journey to repentance captured my attention. In the mid-1800s, Alfred Nobel invented dynamite when he discovered a way to stabilize explosives like no one before him could.

At first dynamite was used mostly for mining purposes and expanding transit across countries. However, because of humanity's seemingly unquenchable need to find creative ways to inflict harm on one another, dynamite became common in war.

Years later, Alfred's brother died. History has retold an apocryphal story of a newspaper that assumed that Alfred himself had died, printing an obituary that condemned him as a "merchant of death."[11]

Alfred was disturbed by the thought of being remembered in such a way. He would later dedicate his resources to the flourishing of humanity through founding the Nobel Prizes.

Hindsight is always good, but there are ways for us to avoid making dangerous contributions to society.

5. Be Content

Oftentimes our desire to grow in prestige leads us to make decisions that are harmful to others. We are so driven by upward mobility that we leave important ethics behind.

> I would rather be what God chose to make me, than the most glorious creature that I could think of. For to have been thought about,—born in God's thoughts,—and then made by God, is the dearest, grandest, most precious thing in all thinking.[12]

This is a heavenly reminder from George MacDonald. What does it mean to find delight in our position? If God has placed us there, then it is the most glorious right place we can be. Romans 12:12 helps us with how to maintain this posture: "Rejoice in hope, be patient in tribulation, be constant in prayer."

I constantly remind myself to live rightly and hold loosely. Things can change, and I must be content with that. It's natural for us to lust for another's platform and position. We are creatures who constantly want to upgrade. We are never satisfied. What makes the gospel other-worldly is that it can make the worrier calm. It can make the lustful fulfilled, and it can make those things that seem undesirable pleasant.

When I was a young athlete, I used to write "Philippians 4:13" on my towel. My hope was that this reference would somehow move me toward greatness. Little did I know I misunderstood this text like many other Christian athletes.

When Paul wrote this letter, he was enduring unpleasant circumstances. He was letting the church of Philippi know that he had experience in a diversity of situations. He'd been hungry and he'd had plenty. He said in verse 11, "I have learned in whatever situation I am to be content." He then moved on to state that he'd learned the secret of contentment. That secret is verse 13: "I can do all things through him who strengthens me."

This is not a text that will help you score more touch-downs. It is a text that will keep you joyful when you are in a scoring drought. This is not a text that will force God to promote you, but it is a text that will help you deal with rejection. No matter my condition, I'm good because I know my place in the economy of God.

Whatever God calls us to, we must consider it good. At the end of the journey, we will find that our hearts were worrying for no reason. Worry added no years to our lives, nor did it slow down our heart rate. In Paulo Coelho's *The Alchemist,* the alchemist shares wise words with the sojourning boy about his fear of suffering:

Tell your heart that the fear of suffering is worse than the suffering itself. And that no heart has ever suffered when it goes in search of its dreams, because every second of the search is a second's encounter with God and with eternity.[13]

6. Seek Rest

This next element is a natural progression from the previous element of contentment. When we are content, we are trusting God in any circumstance. This trust will lead us to rest. Rest is revolutionary in today's progress-absorbed society.

There's a stark difference between laziness and rest. Laziness seeks distraction. Rest requires reflection and peace. Laziness is the refusal to take initiative. Rest intentionally takes the initiative to restore what has been poured out of you. This is beneficial for your whole being.

Many times we refuse to Sabbath because we are afraid to lose relevance. This is a lack of trust in God and our own ability. We must be vigilant to care for our bodies and challenge our industries to care about our bodies as well.

Mental health has never been more in the forefront of society's consciousness than it is today. It's the prisoner's dilemma we live in. We are more diligent to talk about our mental health, but we talk about it because we are overworked and overstimulated. Rest means unplugging.

Journalist Laurie Segall captured the dark side of success while covering Silicon Valley in her CNN docuseries *Mostly Human*. One of the interviewees said,

It's almost like a badge of honor to show how busy you are. Sleep is not cool, pregnancy, not cool. All these things that normal human beings do and need—people need families, they need to go to sleep at night, but somehow that is excluded from the acceptable portion of the culture.[14]

Along with the success and high-paying jobs come high rates of suicide and mental health problems.

In Gabriel García Márquez's fictional masterpiece *One Hundred Years of Solitude,* the city of Macondo is struck with an insomnia plague. What seemed to be a plague is quickly celebrated as a blessing. Because the residents can't sleep, they're able to get an abundance of work done. However, the lack of sleep has repercussions. The people of Macondo begin to lose their memory. They begin to forget how to spell basic words. The brain can't continue to operate without resting.

The narrator points out something else that was lost during the plague. Some of the people found that they missed dreaming.[15] A lack of rest kills creativity.

I have friends and fans who often ask me why I seem to fall off the earth for long spells of time. My absence is not because I have nothing to say. If you know me, then you know I love to hear myself speak. Society is not deficient in giving us opportunities to share our thoughts. I don't want to be a person who knows everything but understands nothing, who is constantly talking and hardly reflecting. That kind of person may have a lot of information but not a lot of wisdom.

Therefore, I disappear for three reasons: to gain wisdom, to keep my sanity, and to live. Many of us have forgotten how to live because we are so busy trying to impress others. Unfortunately, creatives are indoctrinated with the need to remain relevant within our vocations. I've come to learn that relevance isn't based on how much you speak. It's measured by how much people listen when you speak. Is there gravity to your words?

Life is made up of peaks and valleys, and the need to stay on top of the mountain is constantly impressed upon artists. However, when you visit the peak of a mountain, you quickly learn that nothing grows up there. Growth happens in the valley. We should ascend the mountain for exercise and recreation, but it's no place to live.

When individuals spend their lives attempting to stay at the top, they tend to lose a bit of connection with the rest of the world, where life is taking place. Therefore, their work loses authenticity and rootedness. Influence, which isn't always the goal, isn't always about who is the most active or present. It's also about who is paying attention. Who listens? Who has the courage to retreat and rest?

When we're running on fumes and not the power of God, Howard Thurman's note on prayer reminds us of our need to rest and reflect:

> The basic proposition underlying our need for prayer is this: We wish never to be left, literally, to our own resources. Again and again, we discover that our own resources are not equal to the demands of our living.[16]

I've learned that when I'm constantly focused on being relevant, three things happen: (1) Relevance becomes my god. (2) I don't truly believe my talents will make room for me. (3) My work is lazy and generic.

In Exodus 35, Moses said that those who didn't observe the Sabbath would be put to death.[17] Let this be a metaphorical rebuke to us today when we find ourselves disregarding rest in pursuit of relevance. A lack of rest can lead to death.

7. Pursue Excellence

The last element refers to the creative process and not necessarily the end product. I don't promote the idea that Christians deserve to be the best because they believe in God. However, we should give the best effort because of whom we serve. Excellence isn't promised in the product, but it's in the attempt.

George Washington Carver discovered his affinity for science because he first had an affinity for God and the Bible. Seeking God doesn't guarantee an excellent result, but it does increase your effort.

We should never be afraid to succeed. The dangers that come with success are common to every person. We shouldn't be afraid to fail. What is worse than failure is to succeed while mocking the character of God.

I hope that the reader of this book finds great success and wealth. However, I also hope that you understand the difference between biblical excellence and worldly greatness. Worldly greatness is measured by things like wealth and fame. You can be a terrible person and have wealth and fame. Many successful people are terrible to others, selfish with their resources and achievements. Many trail-blazers run over people while they are changing culture.

Biblical excellence is measured by character, love, joy, and service, while success is measured by dollar signs. Excellence has no dollar value to it. There is no earthly exchange rate for a life that is sacrificial.

Jesus said they will know us by our love.[18] I'm afraid many Christians would rather be known for what they know. Knowledge and prestige have an expiration date. Excellence lives beyond your death.

Along with his impact, discoveries, and patents, George Washington Carver left behind a reputation that exemplifies biblical success. His tombstone reads,

> A life that stood out as a gospel of self-forgetting service. He could have added fortune to fame but caring for neither he found happiness and honor in being helpful to the world.

Joseph was helpful to the world because he understood God's call for his life no matter the obstacles in front of him. He knew the Lord's promises and that his calling was greater than his afflictions. The ex-convict Joseph could have added fortune to fame, but caring for neither, he found happiness and honor in becoming a blessing to nations and those who despitefully used him.

Moses found himself to be inadequate for service. The

Lord found him to be enough. This boy was fished out of a river and raised as royalty, only to forsake that position and face an oppressive pharaoh to liberate his people. This liberator could have added fortune to fame, but caring for neither, he found happiness and honor in being a shepherd of God's flock.

Esther knew she wasn't given a platform for her own benefit. Being filled with wisdom and compassion, she put her life at risk for her people. This queen could have added fortune to fame, but caring for neither, she found happiness and honor in leveraging her life for the safety of others.

Daniel excelled in a foreign land. This exiled Hebrew boy wouldn't allow lions or idolatrous decrees to keep him from being devoted to his God. This outcast could have added fortune to fame, but caring for neither, he found happiness and honor in being a man who wouldn't defile the covenant in his heart.

Coming down to earth to offer righteousness to people who didn't deserve it, the Messiah took on sin he didn't commit all to reunite us with God. However, to be reunited with God involves more than our intellectual understanding of salvation. This redemption grabs every idea, every action, every ability and demands that it be submitted to the authority of God. It demands the transformation of whatever doesn't represent his glory.

God is redeeming the things we feel and the things unseen. He will bring into submission the principalities of the world, the kingdoms that reign on high, and the powers that abuse the weak. He heals the brokenness in relationships, the perversion in our work, and the wounds from our past. He is supreme over all, and no cultivation happens outside his knowledge. There is no corruption that will go unpunished. There is no heart that will beat without his authority. Every breath is a mercy. He is a God that operates outside our comprehension, but he is intimate and compassionate. He hates sin but loves the fallen. He is holy, holy, holy. He is a good God with good gifts. If we find him to be unsatisfying, then we don't know what is good.

We should feel so lucky to join him in this act of redemption. It is our privilege to forsake fortune and fame and find happiness and honor in being helpful to the world. This is "on earth as it is in heaven."[19] Oh, what a glorious day it will be when we are no longer clumsy in our redemption. On that day, redemption will have no name because there will be no need for her.

In a moment, time will have no significance and we will see with correct vision. Purity will cloak him as a robe. Praise will drip from his crown. The foundation will applaud every step. Peace will be his aroma, and we will know joy like never before. Our heads will be lifted by love. Our smiles will testify of our satisfaction.

On that day, our eyes will be opened and we shall see for the first time.

We will finally know without doubt—and all creation shall affirm—that *he* is good.

ACKNOWLEDGMENTS

Much love to my agent, Andrew Wolgemuth, for his patience with me in this process. Thank you to my editor, Paul Pastor. I couldn't ask for a better human to wield the red pen over my work.

To my lovely wife, Patreece. You give me the liberating spirit to paint the world as I see it. I love you.

To my mother: there is no single human as strong and sacrificing as you. Your life needs a book. Salute to my siblings—Reggie, Dhati, and Vanja—who molded the imagination of a young kid with music, sports, imaginary play, and board games. I love you guys so much.

To Grandmommy. Thank you for showing me the embodiment of sacrifice and strength. I hope Kanye and Kim make it for your viewing pleasure. However, don't hold your breath, as you used to tell me.

Grandest of affections to my Ace, Nasia Danielle, for her support and ear while I was writing this book. That novel is next, boss lady, and I don't care what Andrew says.

Thanks to the institutions and people who have helped me think more deeply and write more critically: AND Campaign, Humble Beast, Reach Records, Blueprint Church, Forth District, Tearfund USA, Adam Thomason, Shaun Sorrells, Paul Denard, Jon Parker, Bruce Wyche,

Julian Maha, and my Zambian, Zimbo, and South African friends. And thanks to all my Tuskegee University and University North Texas family who cultivated me into the man I am today.

Last, and with most importance, this book is dedicated to all the teachers who told me I'd "never amount to nothin'." To all the people who lived in the buildings that I was hustlin' in front of. Those who called the police on me when I was just tryin' to make some money to feed my daughter. It's all good, baby baby . . .

NOTES

INTRODUCTION *THE GOOD LIFE*

The epigraph is from Erykah Badu, "Tyrone," *Didn't Cha Know,* Motown Records, 2001.

1. Micah 6:8.
2. Luke 10:27.
3. *Encyclopaedia Britannica,* s.v. "Shaka: Zulu Chief," www .britannica.com/biography/Shaka-Zulu-chief.
4. Gilbert K. Chesterton, "The Unmilitary Suffragette," in *What's Wrong with the World* (New York: Dodd, Mead, 1910), 141–45.
5. Alexander Crummell, "The Destined Superiority of the Negro," in *Preaching with Sacred Fire: An Anthology of African American Sermons, 1750 to the Present,* ed. Martha Simmons and Frank A. Thomas (New York: Norton, 2010), 124–26.
6. Gillian Brockell, "'Irresponsible': Historians Attack David Garrow's MLK Allegations," *Washington Post,* May 30, 2019, www.washingtonpost.com/history/2019/05/30/irresponsible -historians-attack-david-garrows-mlk-allegations.
7. W. E. B. Du Bois, "On Stalin," March 16, 1953, Marxists Internet Archive, www.marxists.org/reference/archive/stalin/ biographies/1953/03/16.htm.

1 *YOU LOOK GOOD IN RED*

1. Howard Zinn, *A People's History of the United States: 1492–Present,* 3rd ed. (New York: Routledge, 2013), 8.
2. Genesis 1:26, NET.
3. Genesis 1:31.

4. Sho Baraka, "Kanye, 2009," featuring Jackie Hill Perry, *The Narrative,* Humble Beast Records, 2016.

5. Malcolm Gladwell, *Outliers: The Story of Success* (New York: Little, Brown, 2008), 230–31, 238–39.

6. Frank Smith, *The Book of Learning and Forgetting* (New York: Teachers College Press, 1998), 3.

7. Romans 3:10, NIV.

8. Matthew 19:21, NASB.

9. Donald Bogle, *Toms, Coons, Mulattoes, Mammies, and Bucks: An Interpretive History of Blacks in American Films,* rev. ed. (New York: Bloomsbury Academic, 2016).

10. Carter G. Woodson, *The Mis-Education of the Negro* (Mineola, NY: Dover, 2005), 115.

11. Toni Morrison, "A Humanist View" (lecture, Portland State University, Portland, OR, May 30, 1975), www.mackenzian .com/wp-content/uploads/2014/07/Transcript_PortlandState _TMorrison.pdf, 7.

12. Sketch the Journalist, "S.B.A.F.E.: Sho Baraka Ain't for Everybody," Jam the Hype, February 1, 2013, https://jamthe hype.com/sbafe-sho-baraka-aint-for-everybody.

2 *GOOD CALL*

1. "Strong's H2896—Towb," Blue Letter Bible, www.blueletter bible.org/lang/lexicon/lexicon.cfm?Strongs=H2896&t=KJV.

2. G. K. Chesterton, "The Contented Man," in *A Miscellany of Men* (New York: Dodd, Mead, 1912), 302.

3. Hebrews 10:14, NIV.

4. Exodus 31:2, NLT.

5. Justin Giboney, Michael Wear, and Chris Butler, *Compassion (&) Conviction: The AND Campaign's Guide to Faithful Civic Engagement* (Downers Grove, IL: InterVarsity, 2020), 32.

6. Psalm 19:1.

7. Romans 1:20.

8. Psalm 19:3, NLT.

9. Ecclesiastes 12:13.

3 *GOOD SLAVES, MAD PLANTATIONS*

1. Reggie Williams, "Dietrich Bonhoeffer in the Harlem Renaissance" (lecture, Wheaton College, Wheaton, IL, April 13, 2012), www.youtube.com/watch?v=Bt6kET_qHGE.
2. William Lloyd Garrison, *The Liberator,* March 26, 1852, http://utc.iath.virginia.edu/reviews/rere02at.html.
3. Carl Ellis, "An 'Illiberal' Liberalism: Why Black Folk Can't Get Ahead," The Witness, June 28, 2013, https://thewitness bcc.com/an-illiberal-liberalism-why-black-folk-cant-get -ahead.
4. "David Walker: 1796–1830," Africans in America, PBS, www .pbs.org/wgbh/aia/part4/4p2930.html.
5. David Walker, quoted in Henry Highland Garnet, "A Brief Sketch of the Life and Character of Henry Walker," in David Walker, *Walker's Appeal, with a Brief Sketch of His Life* (New York: J. H. Tobitt, 1848), vii.
6. Walker, *Walker's Appeal,* 55–56.
7. Phillis Wheatley, "On the Death of the Rev. Mr. George Whitefield," in *Complete Writings,* ed. Vincent Carretta (New York: Penguin Books, 2001), 15.
8. Wheatley, "On the Death," 15.
9. Jupiter Hammon, "Address to the Negroes in the State of New York," in *African American Religious History: A Documentary Witness,* ed. Milton C. Sernett, 2nd ed. (Durham, NC: Duke University Press, 1999), 39.
10. Phillis Wheatley, "On the Death of General Wooster," in *Complete Writings,* 93.
11. 1 Timothy 4:1, Voice.
12. James H. Cone, *The Spirituals and the Blues: An Interpretation* (Maryknoll, NY: Orbis Books, 1992), 14.
13. Toni Morrison, "The Individual Artist," in *The Source of Self-Regard: Selected Essays, Speeches, and Meditations* (New York: Vintage International, 2020), 63.

4 *GUD FOLKS DIS'GREE TOO*

1. *Merriam-Webster,* s.v. "gentrification," www.merriam-webster .com/dictionary/gentrification.

2. *I Am Not Your Negro,* directed by Raoul Peck, ARTE et al., 2016.

3. Harold Cruse, *The Crisis of the Negro Intellectual: A Historical Analysis of the Failure of Black Leadership* (New York: New York Review Books, 2005), 58.

4. Devon W. Carbado and Donald Weise, introduction to *Time on Two Crosses: The Collected Writings of Bayard Rustin,* ed. Devon W. Carbado and Donald Weise (San Francisco: Cleis, 2003), xxvi.

5. Thomas C. Oden, *How Africa Shaped the Christian Mind: Rediscovering the African Seedbed of Western Christianity* (Downers Grove, IL: IVP Books, 2007), 69.

6. Toni Morrison, "Faulkner and Women," in *The Source of Self-Regard: Selected Essays, Speeches, and Meditations* (New York: Vintage International, 2020), 300.

7. James Weldon Johnson, quoted in Cruse, *Crisis of the Negro Intellectual,* 21.

8. Lydia Saad, "Black Americans Want Police to Retain Local Presence," Gallup, August 5, 2020, https://news.gallup.com/poll/316571/black-americans-police-retain-local-presence.aspx.

9. Zora Neale Hurston, *Their Eyes Were Watching God* (New York: Harper Perennial, 2006), 16.

10. Hurston, *Their Eyes,* 75.

11. John McWhorter, *Talking Back, Talking Black* (Talks at Google, January 4, 2018), www.youtube.com/watch?v=eoWGx060lyA.

12. Hurston, *Their Eyes,* 68.

13. Anna Julia Cooper, *A Voice from the South* (Xenia, OH: Aldine Printing House, 1892), 149.

14. Hurston, *Their Eyes,* 188.

15. Jeremiah 29:7.

5　THE GOOD EXILES

1. "What Is an Evangelical?," National Association of Evangelicals, www.nae.net/what-is-an-evangelical; D. W. Bebbington, *Evangelicalism in Modern Britain: A History from the 1730s to the 1980s* (London: Unwin Hyman, 1989), 2–3.

2. Jeremiah 29:7.
3. Jeremiah 29:5–6.
4. Exodus 3:7–8, NLT.
5. Exodus 4:22–23, NLT.
6. The Cross Movement, "Blood Spilla'," *Heaven's Mentality,* Cross Movement Records, 1997.
7. The Cross Movement, "Cypha' Time," *Heaven's Mentality,* Cross Movement Records, 1997.
8. Tom Skinner, "The U.S. Racial Crisis and World Evangelism" (lecture, Urbana Student Missions Conference, University of Illinois at Urbana-Champaign, December 1970), https:// urbana.org/message/us-racial-crisis-and-world-evangelism.
9. Carl Ellis Jr., interview by the author, May 13, 2020.
10. "Blacks Make Assault on Moral Decay," *Indianapolis Recorder,* July 12, 1975, 16, https://newspapers.library.in.gov/cgi-bin/ indiana?a=d&d=INR19750712-01.1.16&e=————-en-20 –1—txt-txIN———.
11. Thomas Fritz, interview by the author, May 2020.
12. Tom Skinner, "Racism Still Divides Black and White America," interview, The Center for Public Justice, May–June 1991, www.cpjustice.org/public/page/content/racism_still _divides.
13. Harold Cruse, *The Crisis of the Negro Intellectual: A Historical Analysis of the Failure of Black Leadership* (New York: New York Review Books, 2005), 80.
14. *Encyclopedia of the Harlem Renaissance,* ed. Cary D. Wintz and Paul Finkelman, vol. 2, *K–Y,* s.v. "Lincoln Theater" (New York: Routledge, 2004), 695–96.
15. Cruse, *Crisis of the Negro Intellectual,* 56–58.
16. Cruse, *Crisis of the Negro Intellectual,* 61.
17. Cruse, *Crisis of the Negro Intellectual,* 65.
18. James H. Cone, *The Spirituals and the Blues: An Interpretation* (Maryknoll, NY: Orbis Books, 1992), 95.
19. Cone, *Spirituals and the Blues,* 95.

6 *LIGHT WORDS IN A GOOD NIGHT*

1. Bradford William Davis, "Southern Baptist Retailer Removes Black Hip-Hop Artist's Album That includes the Word 'Penis,'" *Washington Post,* February 8, 2017, www.washington post.com/news/acts-of-faith/wp/2017/02/08/southern-baptist -retailer-removes-black-hip-hop-artists-album-that-includes -the-word-penis.
2. Henry James, preface to *The Portrait of a Lady,* ed. Roger Luckhurst (Oxford: Oxford University Press, 2009), 7.
3. Flannery O'Connor, "Some Aspects of the Grotesque in Southern Fiction," in *Mystery and Manners: Occasional Prose,* ed. Sally Fitzgerald and Robert Fitzgerald (New York: Farrar, Straus & Giroux, 1970), 44.
4. Ecclesiastes 7:1–4, NLT.
5. Darryl Ford, "Funerals, Church Hurt, and the Beyoncé Standard," episode 2, February 27, 2020, in *The Sho Baraka Show,* podcast, 37:00, www.spreaker.com/user/forthdistrict/ shoshow2-24-20-mixdown-mp3edit1.
6. *The Dark Knight Rises,* directed by Christopher Nolan (Burbank, CA: Warner Bros. Entertainment, 2012).
7. John 17:15–18, CSB.
8. Ivana Parker, email message to the author, 2020.
9. Romans 8:28: "We know that for those who love God all things work together for good, for those who are called according to his purpose."

7 *YOU GOOD?*

1. Romans 12:1–2, CSB.
2. George Washington Carver, *George Washington Carver in His Own Words,* ed. Gary R. Kremer, 2nd ed. (Columbia, MO: University of Missouri Press, 2017), 24.
3. George Washington Carver, quoted in Glenn Clark, *The Man Who Talks with the Flowers: The Intimate Life Story of Dr. George Washington Carver* (Hoboken, NJ: Start Publishing, 2012), chap. 1.
4. George Washington Carver, quoted in John Perry, *Unshakable*

Faith: Booker T. Washington & George Washington Carver (Sisters, OR: Multnomah, 1999), 315.

5. Jim Hardwick, quoted in Clark, *Man Who Talks,* chap. 1.
6. George Washington Carver, in *The Essential Writings of the American Black Church,* ed. John Hunt (Chattanooga, TN: AMG, 2008), 688.
7. Romans 12:3, CSB.
8. C. S. Lewis, *The Great Divorce: A Dream* (New York: Harper-Collins, 2001), 40.
9. Mark 9:35.
10. *Do the Right Thing,* directed by Spike Lee, Forty Acres and a Mule Filmworks, 1989.
11. Evan Andrews, "Did a Premature Obituary Inspire the Nobel Prize?," History.com, updated July 23, 2020, www.history .com/news/did-a-premature-obituary-inspire-the-nobel-prize.
12. George MacDonald, *David Elginbrod* (New York: George Routledge & Sons, n.d.), 238–39.
13. Paulo Coelho, *The Alchemist,* 25th anniversary ed. (New York: HarperOne, 2014), 134.
14. Rand Fishkin, quoted in "Silicon Valley's Secret," *Mostly Human,* CNNMoney, https://money.cnn.com/mostly-human/ silicon-valleys-secret.
15. Gabriel García Márquez, *One Hundred Years of Solitude,* trans. Gregory Rabassa (New York: Harper Perennial, 2006), 45.
16. Howard Thurman, "Lord, Teach Us to Pray," in *Preaching with Sacred Fire: An Anthology of African American Sermons, 1750 to the Present,* ed. Martha Simmons and Frank A. Thomas (New York: Norton, 2010), 576.
17. Exodus 35:2.
18. John 13:35.
19. Matthew 6:10.

ABOUT THE AUTHOR

Sho Baraka is actually Amisho Baraka Lewis, who attended Tuskegee University and the University of North Texas. When he's not doing amazing stuff like making hot music, writing, acting, giving lectures, or globe-trotting as an activist and culture curator, he is probably reminiscing about old music with his wife, exchanging quips with his daughter, or being a human pillow for his boys.

Follow Sho Baraka at @amishobaraka
on all platforms.

www.barakaology.com